W9-BYB-120

A FESTIVE CHRISTMAS
IN PLASTIC CANVAS

What a perfect partnership — plastic canvas and the Yuletide season! For a holly-jolly holiday, *spark* your decorating and gift-giving with the oodles of ornaments, clever centerpieces, and *appealing* accents in A Festive Christmas in Plastic Canvas. Oh, what fun it is to pick and choose from more *than* 60 top-quality, one-of-a-kind projects! You'll love the sleighful of Santas, snowmen, angels, and *more*. Stitchers of all skill levels will catch the joyous spirit, whether crafting at the last minute (*many items* are a whiz to whip up!) or with time to spare. So don't delay — gather your gear and *begin* today to prepare a plastic canvas celebration for every nook and cranny of your house!

LEISURE ARTS, INC.
and
OXMOOR HOUSE, INC.

A FESTIVE CHRISTMAS
IN PLASTIC CANVAS

EDITORIAL STAFF

Vice President and Editor-in-Chief:
 Anne Van Wagner Childs
Executive Director: Sandra Graham Case
Editorial Director: Susan Frantz Wiles
Publications Director: Carla Bentley
Creative Art Director: Gloria Bearden
Senior Graphics Art Director: Melinda Stout

PRODUCTION
Special Projects Editor: Donna Brown Hill
Project Coordinator: Mary Sullivan Hutcheson
Senior Production Assistant: JoAnn Forrest
Project Assistants: Lylln Craig, Christine Street,
 and Janie Wright

EDITORIAL
Managing Editor: Linda L. Trimble
Associate Editor: Janice Teipen Wojcik
Editorial Associates: Terri Leming Davidson and
 Stacey Robertson Marshall

DESIGN
Design Director: Patricia Wallenfang Sowers

ART
Crafts Art Director: Rhonda Hodge Shelby
Senior Production Artist: Katie Murphy
Production Artists: Keith Melton, Brent Miller,
 Dana Vaughn, Mary Ellen Wilhelm, and
 Karen L. Wilson
Photography Stylists: Beth Carter, Pam Choate,
 Aurora Huston, Laura Reed, and Courtney Jones

PROMOTIONS
Managing Editors: Alan Caudle and Marjorie Ann Lacy
Associate Editors: Steven M. Cooper, Dixie L. Morris,
 Jennifer Ertl Wobser, Ellen J. Clifton, and Marie Trotter
Designer: Dale Rowett
Art Director: Linda Lovette Smart
Production Artist: Leslie Loring Krebs
Publishing Systems Administrator: Cindy Lumpkin
Publishing Systems Assistants: Susan Mary Gray and
 Robert Walker

BUSINESS STAFF

Publisher: Bruce Akin
Vice President and General Manager:
 Thomas L. Carlisle
Retail Sales Director: Richard Tignor
Vice President, Retail Marketing: Pam Stebbins

Retail Marketing Director: Margaret Sweetin
Retail Customer Services Manager: Carolyn Pruss
General Merchandise Manager: Cathy Laird
Vice President, Finance: Tom Siebenmorgen
Distribution Director: Rob Thieme

A FESTIVE CHRISTMAS IN PLASTIC CANVAS
from the *Plastic Canvas Creations* series
Published by Leisure Arts, Inc., and Oxmoor House, Inc.

Library of Congress Catalog Number 98-65187
Hardcover ISBN 1-57486-129-8
Softcover ISBN 1-57486-067-4

TABLE OF CONTENTS

Heartwarming Santas

Embellished with a curly white beard and gold metallic yarn, this handsome Santa is a heartwarming reminder that Christmas is a season of happiness. A 10 mesh version of this popular patriarch spreads joy to the world as an elegant tree topper (below).

HEARTWARMING SANTAS
TABLETOP DECORATION

Size: 10¼"w x 13¾"h x 2"d

Supplies: Worsted weight yarn, gold metallic braid, two 10½" x 13½" sheets of clear 7 mesh plastic canvas, #16 tapestry needle, polyester fiberfill, white Mini-curl™ doll hair, and craft glue

Stitches Used: Cross Stitch, Double French Knot, Gobelin Stitch, Overcast Stitch, and Tent Stitch

Instructions: Follow charts to cut and stitch pieces. Work Santa Back using red slanting Gobelin Stitches over three threads. Using gold metallic braid, cover unworked edges of Heart pieces.

String hearts together to make a garland. Thread braid through canvas on left hand of Santa Front, then tie a knot on back of canvas. Repeat for right hand.

Using yarn color to match Front, join Santa Front to Back, leaving bottom edges open. Lightly stuff Santa with polyester fiberfill.

For Base, cut two 16 x 16 thread pieces of canvas. Base pieces are not stitched. Using green yarn, stack Base pieces and join to Santa Front at ▲'s through three thicknesses of plastic canvas. Using red yarn, join Base pieces to Santa Back. Glue individual pieces of doll hair to Santa's beard.

TREETOP DECORATION

Size: 7"w x 9¼"h x 1½"d

Supplies: Sport weight yarn, gold metallic braid, two 10½" x 13½" sheets of clear 10 mesh plastic canvas, #20 tapestry needle, white Mini-curl™ doll hair, and craft glue

Stitches Used: Cross Stitch, Double French Knot, Gobelin Stitch, Overcast Stitch, and Tent Stitch

Instructions: Follow charts to cut and stitch pieces. Work Santa Back using red slanting Gobelin Stitches over three threads. Using gold metallic braid, cover unworked edges of Heart pieces.

String hearts together to make a garland. Thread braid through canvas on left hand of Santa Front, then tie a knot on back of canvas. Repeat for right hand.

Using yarn color to match Front, join Santa Front to Back, leaving bottom edges open.

Using green yarn, cover unworked edges between ▲'s on Santa Front. Using red yarn, cover unworked edges on Back. Glue individual pieces of doll hair to Santa's beard.

Design by Joan Green.

✎	white
✎	flesh
✎	gold metallic
✎	pink
✎	red
✎	green
✎	black
●	white Double French Knot
●	red Double French Knot
●	green Double French Knot

Heart #1 (11 x 10 threads)

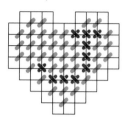

Heart #2 (11 x 10 threads)

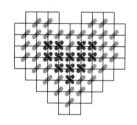

Heart #3 (11 x 10 threads)

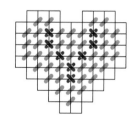

Santa Front/Back
(70 x 91 threads) (cut 2)

7

Santa's Forest Friends

From foxes and bears to skunks and bunnies, Santa and his furry little friends wish you a Merry Christmas! Delicate snowflakes and elegant evergreens add a soft touch to this rustic ornament set, which is stitched on clear, white, and brown canvas.

SANTA'S FOREST FRIENDS

Approx Size: 5"w x 5"h each

Supplies: Worsted weight yarn, two 10½" x 13½" sheets of clear 7 mesh plastic canvas, one 10½" x 13½" sheet of white 7 mesh plastic canvas, one 10½" x 13½" sheet of brown 7 mesh plastic canvas, #16 tapestry needle, nylon line, and craft glue

Stitches Used: Backstitch, Cross Stitch, French Knot, Fringe Stitch, Gobelin Stitch, Overcast Stitch, Tent Stitch, and Turkey Loop Stitch

Instructions: Follow chart to cut Star Ornament pieces from brown plastic canvas. Follow chart to cut Snowflake Ornament from white plastic canvas. Follow charts to cut remaining pieces from clear plastic canvas. Follow charts to stitch pieces. Refer to photo to add red 2-ply French Knots to Fox, Skunk, Rabbit, and Bear pieces.

Glue animals to Ornaments. For hangers, thread 8" of nylon line through top of each Ornament. Tie ends of nylon line into a knot 3" above each stitched piece and trim ends.

Designs by Dick Martin.

white		tan	
ecru		taupe	
cream		brown	
flesh		brown 2-ply	
orange		black	
pink		white 2-ply French Knot	
red		pink 2-ply French Knot	
dk red		red 2-ply French Knot	
lt green		black 2-ply French Knot	
green		lt green Fringe	
rust		lt green Turkey Loop	
beige			

Fox (23 x 15 threads)
Cut 2 from clear canvas.

Squirrel (13 x 12 threads)
Cut 2 from clear canvas.

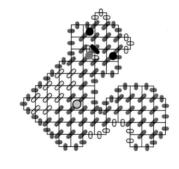

Cardinal
(10 x 11 threads)
Cut 4 from clear canvas.

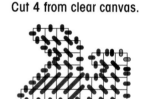

Skunk (15 x 17 threads)
Cut 2 from clear canvas.

Rabbit (12 x 15 threads)
Cut from clear canvas.

Bear (17 x 15 threads)
Cut 2 from clear canvas.

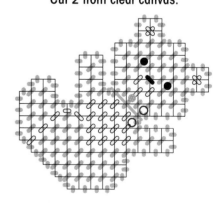

Snowflake Ornament (30 x 30 threads)

Cut from white canvas.

Santa Ornament (32 x 30 threads)

Cut from clear canvas.

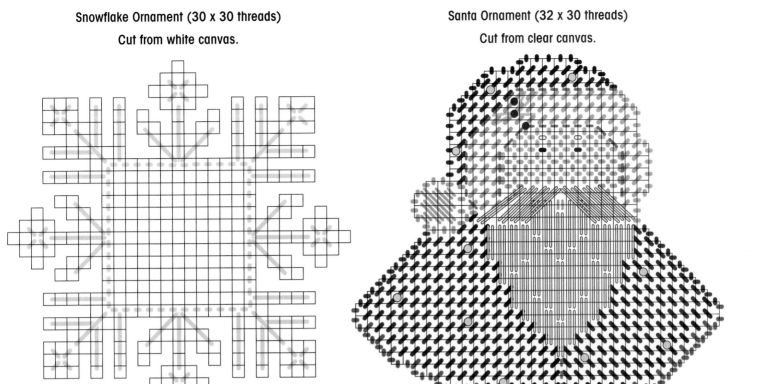

Woodland Ornament (29 x 29 threads)

Cut 4 from clear canvas.

Star Ornament (34 x 34 threads)

Cut 4 from brown canvas.

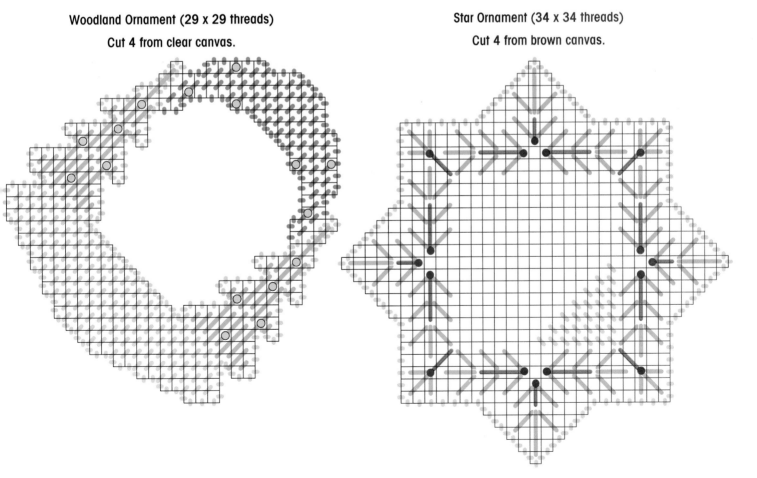

Christmas Tree Music Box

A bright gold star complements the shiny beads on our graceful evergreen music box. The festive strains of your favorite holiday tunes come from a music box hidden beneath the checkered gold metallic and green base.

CHRISTMAS TREE MUSIC BOX

Size: 8³/₄"h x 4" dia

Supplies: Worsted weight yarn, gold metallic braid, one 13¹/₂" x 22" sheet of clear 7 mesh plastic canvas, one Darice® 4¹/₂" plastic canvas circle, #16 tapestry needle, 100 - 6mm gold beads, nylon line, sewing needle (for working with nylon line), 2³/₈" x 2" x 1¹/₄" keywind music box, rotating base to fit music box, and craft glue

Stitches Used: Gobelin Stitch, Mosaic Stitch, Overcast Stitch, and Tent Stitch

Instructions: Follow charts to cut and stitch Music Box Side, Tree Side, and Star pieces, leaving stitches in shaded area unworked. Attach beads to Tree Side using nylon line. Refer to chart to cut Music Box Base from circle along blue cutting line. Stitch Music Box Base.

Using green yarn, join Tree Sides together. Cover unworked edges of Tree.

Matching ✳'s, join Star pieces together using gold metallic braid. Glue Star to top of Tree.

Match ✖'s and work stitches in shaded area to join short ends of Music Box Side together, forming a cylinder. Using gold metallic braid, join Base to Side.

Using nylon line, tack Tree to Music Box Base. Screw rotating base into music box. Center rotating base under stitched piece. Glue music box to wrong side of Music Box Base.

Design by Mary Perry.

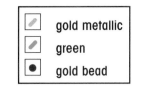

✏	gold metallic
✏	green
●	gold bead

Music Box Base

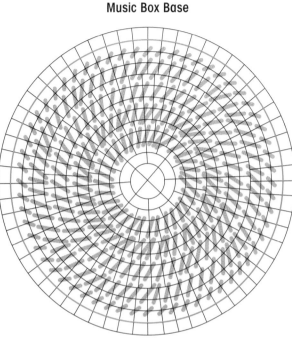

Music Box Side

(14 x 92 threads)

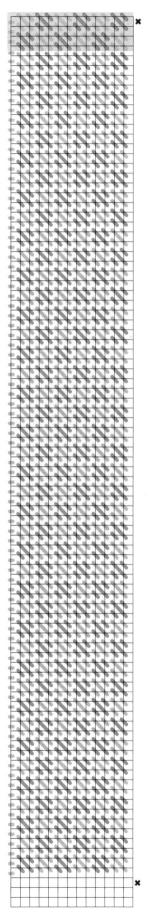

Tree Side (34 x 34 threads)

(stitch 5)

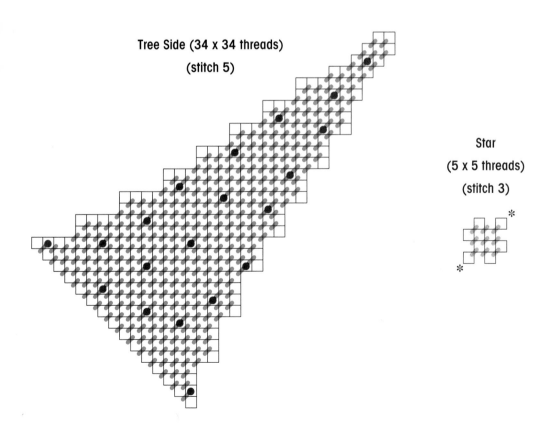

Star

(5 x 5 threads)

(stitch 3)

13

Stunning Poinsettia Set

Brightly colored poinsettias make a stunning centerpiece, especially when clustered with tastefully framed photos. Known as the Flower of the Holy Night in its native Mexico, the poinsettia becomes even more appealing when surrounded with holiday greenery and flourishes. Each leaf is stitched around a floral wire stem so that it can retain its gently curved shape.

STUNNING POINSETTIA SET

CENTERPIECE

Poinsettia Size: 7¹/₂" dia each

Poinsettia Supplies: Worsted weight yarn, gold metallic braid, five 10¹/₂" x 13¹/₂" sheets of clear 7 mesh plastic canvas, five 3" dia plastic canvas circles, #16 tapestry needle, sixty-five 18" lengths of 20 gauge floral wire, and floral tape

Centerpiece Supplies: 10¹/₂"w x 3³/₄"h x 8"d oval container, florist foam, assorted artificial greenery, wire-edge ribbon, artificial gold vine, Spanish moss, artificial gold berry spray, and craft glue

Stitches Used: Double French Knot, French Knot, Gobelin Stitch, Overcast Stitch, and Tent Stitch

Instructions: Follow charts to cut Petal pieces. Fold one length of floral wire in half. Place floral wire on back of one Large Petal along placement line. Follow chart to stitch Large Petal, covering wire as you stitch. Repeat for remaining Large and Small Petal pieces.

For Center, trim six threads from one plastic canvas circle. Follow chart to clip every other thread on edge of circle. Fold one length of wire in half. Insert ends of wire through middle of Center piece and twist wire to hold Center close to fold in wire. Follow chart to stitch green Double French Knots. Work gold French Knot on top of each green Double French Knot. Repeat for remaining Center pieces.

Using floral tape, wrap wires on five Small Petals, seven Large Petals, and one Center piece. Refer to photo to arrange Petals around Center. Wrap wires together with floral tape to hold Petals in place. Repeat to make a total of five Poinsettias.

Insert Poinsettias, greenery, vine, and berries into florist foam. Cover foam with Spanish moss. Tie ribbon into a bow and trim ends. Glue ribbon to Spanish moss.

✏	red
Ⓞ	green Double French Knot
⊙	gold metallic French Knot
✎	wire placement

Small Petal

(6 x 18 threads) (stitch 25)

Large Petal

(22 x 22 threads) (stitch 35)

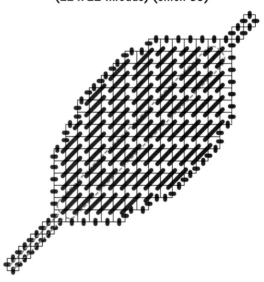

Center

(stitch 5)

PICTURE FRAMES

Small Frame Size: $4^{1}/_{4}$"w x 5"h
(Photo opening is $1^{3}/_{4}$"w x $2^{3}/_{4}$"h.)

Large Frame Size: 5"w x $6^{1}/_{2}$"h
(Photo opening is $2^{3}/_{4}$"w x $4^{1}/_{4}$"h.)

Supplies for One Frame: Worsted weight yarn, gold metallic braid, one $10^{1}/_{2}$" x $13^{1}/_{2}$" sheet of clear 7 mesh stiff plastic canvas, and #16 tapestry needle

Stitches Used: Gobelin Stitch, Overcast Stitch, Smyrna Cross Stitch, and Tent Stitch

Small Frame Instructions: Follow chart to cut and stitch Front. For Back, cut a piece of plastic canvas 28 x 34 threads. For Stand Top, cut a piece of plastic canvas 12 x 34 threads. For Stand Bottom, cut a piece of plastic canvas 12 x 21 threads. Back, Stand Top, and Stand Bottom are not worked.

Refer to Diagram to construct Small Frame. Using green yarn, join Stand Top and Stand Bottom together along short edges. Tack Stand to Back. Join Front to Back along unworked edges of Front. Cover unworked edge of Back.

Large Frame Instructions: Follow chart to cut and stitch Front. For Back, cut a piece of plastic canvas 34 x 44 threads. For Stand Top, cut a piece of plastic canvas 12 x 44 threads. For Stand Bottom, cut a piece of plastic canvas 12 x 21 threads. Back, Stand Top, and Stand Bottom are not worked.

Refer to Diagram to construct Large Frame. Using red yarn, join Stand Top and Stand Bottom together along short edges. Tack Stand to Back. Join Front to Back along unworked edges of Front. Cover unworked edge of Back.

Frame design by Ruby Thacker.

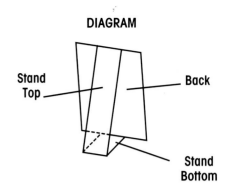

DIAGRAM

Stand Top — Back — Stand Bottom

	gold metallic
	red
	green

Small Frame Front (28 x 34 threads)

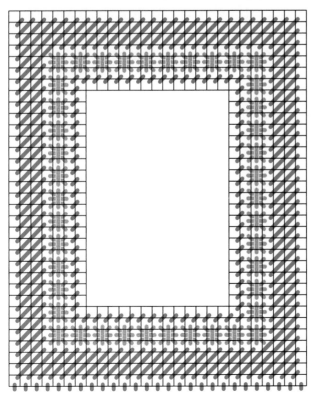

Large Frame Front (34 x 44 threads)

17

Charming Nativity

Our three-dimensional Nativity set is a charming and reverent way to celebrate the holy feast of Christmas. Precious Baby Jesus rests in a free-standing manger, attended by a kneeling Mary, Joseph with staff, and humble farm animals. Worked with embroidery floss on 14 mesh canvas, a dainty version of the set adds an elegant touch to an evergreen wreath.

Santa Bear Candy Keeper

Jolly Santa Bear is "ho-ho-hoing" his way through the Christmas season as a clever candy cane keeper. Embellished with a ribbon bow, gold metallic yarn, and a fur-cuffed stocking, our adorable bear will melt your heart as he offers his treats!

SANTA BEAR CANDY KEEPER

Size: 6³/₄"w x 10¹/₂"h x 3"d

Supplies: Worsted weight yarn, gold metallic braid, two 10¹/₂" x 13¹/₂" sheets of clear 7 mesh stiff plastic canvas, #16 tapestry needle, 2¹/₂"w x 1¹/₄"h piece of white fur, 16" length of ¹/₄"w green satin ribbon, and craft glue

Stitches Used: Alternating Scotch Stitch, Backstitch, Cross Stitch, French Knot, Overcast Stitch, and Tent Stitch

Instructions: Follow charts to cut and stitch pieces. Using matching color yarn, cover unworked edges of Bear.

Glue fur to Stocking. Tie braid into a bow and trim ends. Glue bow to Stocking. Glue Stocking to Bear. Tie green ribbon into a bow and trim ends. Glue ribbon to Bear.

Using green yarn, match long edges and join Box Front to Sides. Join Back to Sides. Join Bottom to Front, Back, and Sides. Glue Bear to Box.

Design by Nancy Dorman.

⟋	white
⟋	red
⟋	dk red
⟋	green
⟋	tan
⟋	brown
⟋	black
⟋	black 2-ply
●	gold metallic French Knot

Bear
(43 x 70 threads)

Stocking

(11 x 19 threads)

Box Side

(17 x 32 threads) (stitch 2)

Box Front/Back

(29 x 32 threads) (stitch 2)

Box Bottom

(29 x 17 threads)

Santa Claus Coaster Set

Jingle all the way to the North Pole and back with Santa in the driver's seat of this delightful coaster holder! Tiny sleigh bells embellish six Santa coasters and the edge of our gold-trimmed sleigh.

SANTA CLAUS COASTER SET

Sleigh Size: 8¼"w x 3¼"h x 2¾"d
Coaster Size: 4½"w x 5½"h
Supplies: Worsted weight yarn, 18" length of gold metallic trim, sixteen ³⁄₈" gold jingle bells, three 10½" x 13½" sheets of clear 7 mesh plastic canvas, #16 tapestry needle, and craft glue
Stitches Used: Alicia Lace Stitch, Backstitch, Cross Stitch, Gobelin Stitch, Overcast Stitch, Tent Stitch, and Turkey Loop Stitch
Instructions: Follow charts to cut and stitch pieces, leaving stitches in shaded areas unworked. Using white yarn, cover unworked edges of Sleigh Bottom, leaving stitches in shaded areas unworked.
Matching ♣'s and ✝'s, join Sleigh Front to Side A using matching color yarn. Matching ♦'s and ♥'s, join Back to Side B. Join remaining unworked edges of Front and Back pieces to Sides.
Matching ★'s and ■'s, work stitches in shaded area to join Sleigh Side A to Bottom. Matching ✳'s and ▲'s, work stitches in shaded area to join Side B to Bottom.
Glue trim and ten bells to Sleigh. Glue one bell to each Santa.

Design by Jack Peatman for LuvLee.

⁄	white
⁄	flesh
⁄	pink
⁄	red
⁄	dk red 2-ply
⁄	blue
⁄	green
⁄	grey
⁄	black
O	white Turkey Loop

Santa
(30 x 35 threads) (stitch 6)

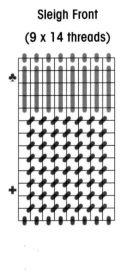

Sleigh Front
(9 x 14 threads)

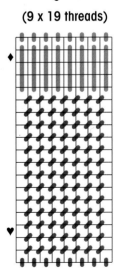

Sleigh Back
(9 x 19 threads)

Continued on page 34

Sleigh Side A (44 x 20 threads)

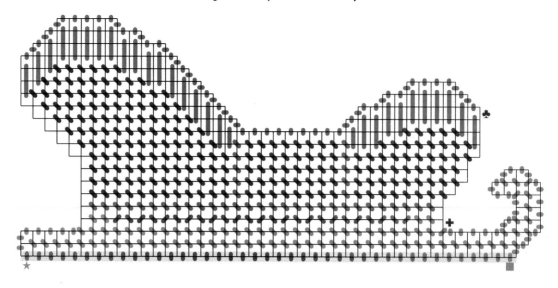

Sleigh Side B (44 x 20 threads)

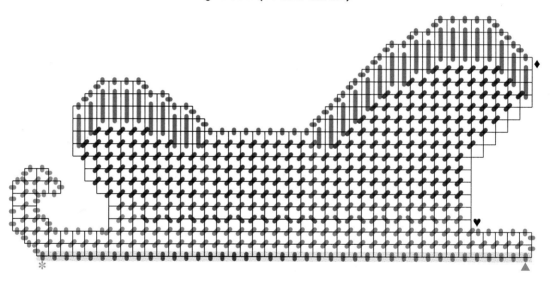

Sleigh Bottom (55 x 19 threads)

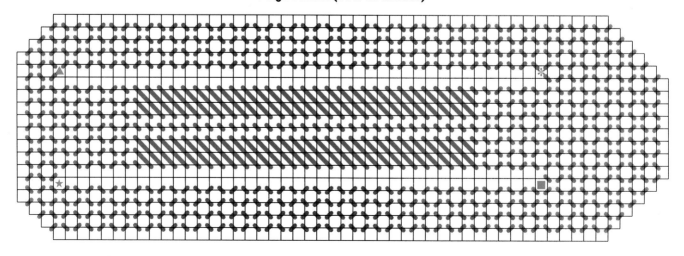

34

Package Ornaments

Wrap up your Christmas tree by putting pretty packages on the branches instead of beneath them! Accented with poinsettias or evergreens, each of these ornaments is topped with a perky three-loop bow.

PACKAGE ORNAMENTS

Size: 3¼"w x 4½"h x ½"d each

Supplies for One Ornament: Worsted weight yarn, one 10½" x 13½" sheet of clear 7 mesh plastic canvas, #16 tapestry needle, and nylon line

Stitches Used: Backstitch, French Knot, Modified Lazy Daisy Stitch, Overcast Stitch, and Tent Stitch

Instructions: Follow charts to cut and stitch pieces. Using white yarn, cover unworked edges of Loop pieces. Using matching color yarn, join Front to Back.

Matching ◆'s and ★'s, fold short ends of Bottom Loop and tack in place using white yarn. Fold Top Loop in half and tack to Bottom Loop. Center and tack bow to top of Ornament.

For hanger, thread 8" of nylon line through Top Loop. Tie ends into a knot 3" above Ornament and trim ends.

Designs by Mary T. Cosgrove.

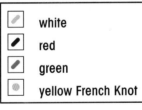

white
red
green
yellow French Knot

Top Loop

(18 x 3 threads)

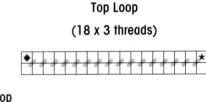

Bottom Loop

(42 x 3 threads)

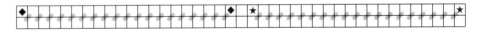

Tree Ornament Front/Back

(21 x 21 threads) (stitch 2)

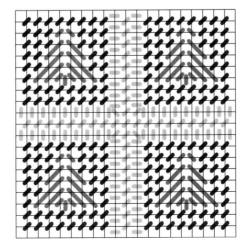

Poinsettia Ornament Front/Back

(21 x 21 threads) (stitch 2)

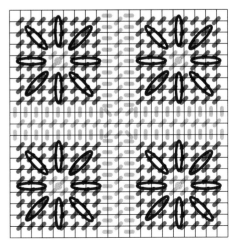

Gilded Ensemble

Gilded with gold beads and metallic thread, this geometric ensemble is a creative way to bring holiday spirit into your home. Keep the entire set — a boutique tissue box cover, a card tray, and potpourri cubes — to spruce up your own house, or share an item or two with the lucky folks on your gift list.

GILDED ENSEMBLE
TISSUE BOX COVER

Size: 4³/₄"w x 5¹/₂"h x 4³/₄"d
(Fits a 4¹/₄"w x 5¹/₄"h x 4¹/₄"d boutique tissue box.)

Supplies: Worsted weight yarn, gold metallic braid, two 10¹/₂" x 13¹/₂" sheets of white 7 mesh plastic canvas, #16 tapestry needle, sixty-four 4mm gold beads, nylon line, and sewing needle (for working with nylon line)

Stitches Used: Cross Stitch, Gobelin Stitch, Overcast Stitch, and Tent Stitch

Instructions: Follow charts to cut and stitch pieces. Attach beads to pieces using nylon line.

Using matching color yarn, join Sides together along long edges. Using red yarn, join Top to Sides.

CARD HOLDER

Size: 8³/₄"w x 2¹/₂"h x 7³/₄"d

Supplies: Worsted weight yarn, gold metallic braid, two 10¹/₂" x 13¹/₂" sheets of white 7 mesh plastic canvas, #16 tapestry needle, thirty 4mm gold beads, nylon line, and sewing needle (for working with nylon line)

Stitches Used: Cross Stitch, Gobelin Stitch, Overcast Stitch, and Tent Stitch

Instructions: Follow charts to cut and stitch pieces. Attach beads to pieces using nylon line.

Using matching color yarn, join Sides together to form a box, alternating Side #1 and Side #2 pieces. Cut a 59 x 52 thread piece of canvas for Box Bottom. Bottom is not stitched. Using red yarn, join Bottom to Sides.

POTPOURRI CUBE

Size: 2¹/₂" cube

Supplies for One Cube: Worsted weight yarn, gold metallic braid, one 10¹/₂" x 13¹/₂" sheet of white 7 mesh plastic canvas, twenty-four 4mm gold beads, #16 tapestry needle, nylon line, sewing needle (for working with nylon line), and potpourri

Stitches Used: Cross Stitch, Overcast Stitch, and Tent Stitch

Instructions: Follow charts to cut and stitch pieces. Attach beads to pieces using nylon line.

Using red yarn, join five Sides together. Fill Cube with potpourri. Join remaining Side to Cube. For hanger, thread 8" of nylon line through top of Cube. Tie ends of nylon line into a knot 3" above Cube and trim ends.

Designs by Ann Townsend.

	gold metallic
	red
	green
●	gold bead

Tissue Box Cover Side

(31 x 37 threads) (stitch 4)

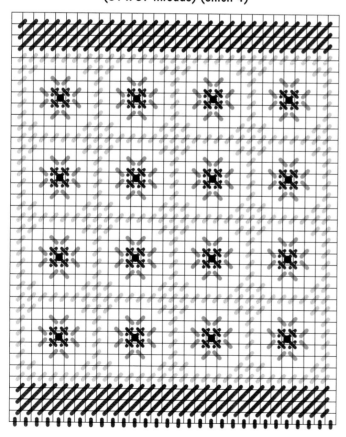

Tissue Box Cover Top

(31 x 31 threads)

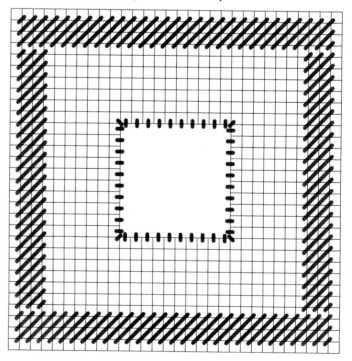

Potpourri Cube Side

(17 x 17 threads) (stitch 6)

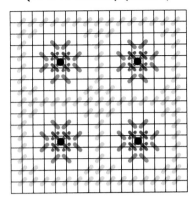

Card Holder Side #1

(52 x 16 threads) (stitch 2)

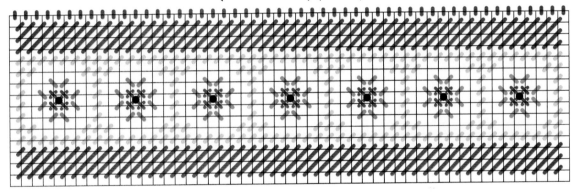

Card Holder Side #2

(59 x 16 threads) (stitch 2)

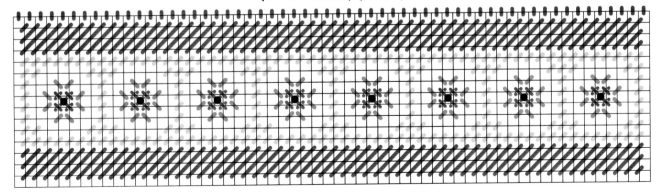

39

Traditional Tree Trims

Bring the spirited appeal of traditional Yuletide characters into your home with our delightful 10-piece ornament set. From a toy-toting Santa to a trumpeting angel, these handsomely detailed designs sprinkle nostalgia and excitement on many different spots — the tree, an evergreen garland, a wreath, or holiday packages.

TRADITIONAL TREE TRIMS

Approx Size: 3³/₄"w x 4"h each

Supplies for One Ornament: Worsted weight yarn, one 10¹/₂" x 13¹/₂" sheet of clear 7 mesh plastic canvas, #16 tapestry needle, and nylon line

Stitches Used: Backstitch, Cross Stitch, French Knot, Gobelin Stitch, Overcast Stitch, Tent Stitch, and Turkey Loop Stitch

Instructions: Follow charts to cut and stitch desired Ornament. Using matching color yarn, cover unworked edges of stitched piece. For hanger, thread 8" of nylon line through top of Ornament. Tie ends of nylon line into a knot 3" above Ornament and trim ends.

Designs by Barbara Baatz.

⟋	white
⟋	flesh
⟋	red
⟋	purple
⟋	blue
⟋	lt green
⟋	green
⟋	tan
⟋	brown
⟋	grey
⟋	grey 2-ply
⟋	black
⟋	gold metallic
●	orange French Knot
◉	pink French Knot
●	red French Knot
●	blue French Knot
●	black French Knot
●	black 2-ply French Knot

Angel
(30 x 29 threads)

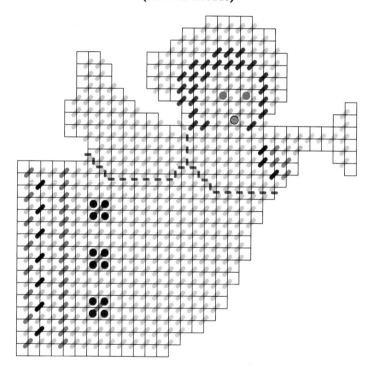

Snowman
(27 x 28 threads)

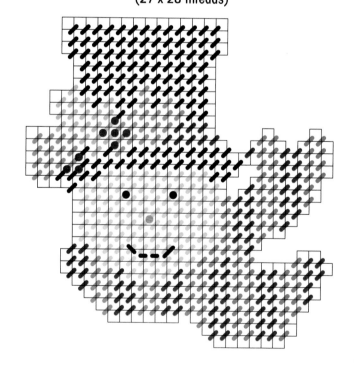

Bell
(27 x 30 threads)

Santa With Tree
(26 x 30 threads)

Candy Cane
(17 x 30 threads)

Rocking Horse
(30 x 30 threads)

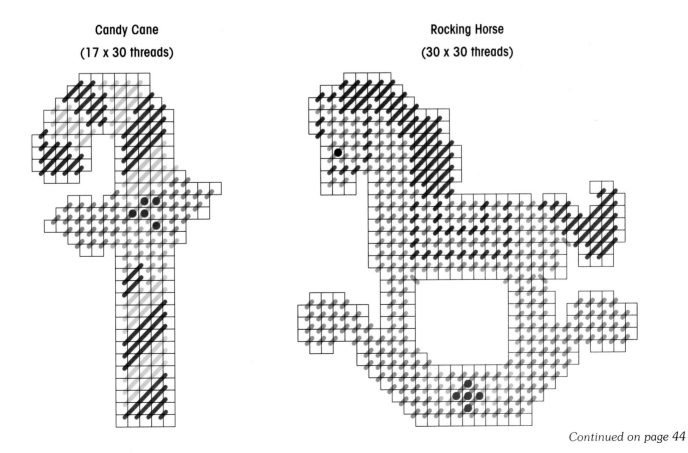

Continued on page 44

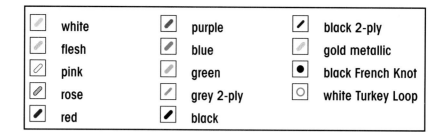

	white		purple		black 2-ply
	flesh		blue		gold metallic
	pink		green	●	black French Knot
	rose		grey 2-ply	○	white Turkey Loop
	red		black		

Santa Face

(26 x 26 threads)

Toy Soldier

(16 x 30 threads)

Stocking

(20 x 29 threads)

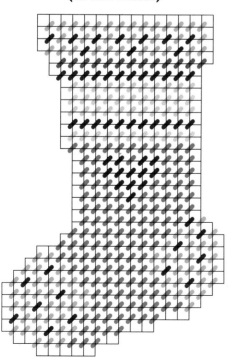

Train

(29 x 22 threads)

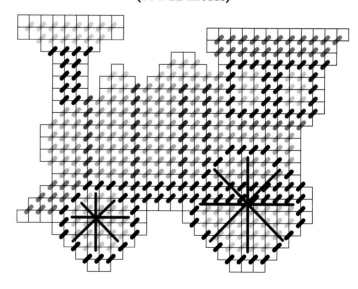

Santa Photo Frame

Picture your favorite little Santa in our quick-and-easy photo keeper! This super-fast frame makes a charming gift, stocking stuffer, or special package decoration.

SANTA PHOTO FRAME

Size: 3³/₄"w x 3³/₄"h
(Photo opening is 1¹/₈"w x 1¹/₈"h.)

Supplies: Worsted weight yarn, one 10¹/₂" x 13¹/₂" sheet of clear 7 mesh plastic canvas, #16 tapestry needle, nylon line, sewing needle (for working with nylon line), and craft glue

Stitches Used: Backstitch, Overcast Stitch, and Tent Stitch

Instructions: Follow chart to cut and stitch Front. Using matching color yarn, cover unworked edges of Front. Glue photo to back of Front.

For Stand Top, cut a piece of plastic canvas 5 x 21 threads. For Stand Bottom, cut a piece of plastic canvas 5 x 14 threads. Stand Top and Stand Bottom are not worked.

Using red yarn, join Stand Top and Stand Bottom together along one short edge of each piece. Using nylon line, tack Stand Bottom to bottom edge of Front. Tack Stand Top to back of Front.

Design by Mary T. Cosgrove.

Front
(25 x 25 threads)

⬭	white
⬭	red
⬭	green
⬭	black

Joyful Angel Banner

Proclaiming "Joy to the World," our angelic banner welcomes Christmas visitors with a message of goodwill. Fashioned in festive red, green, and gold, this eye-catching piece sets a holiday tone for your entire house.

JOYFUL ANGEL BANNER

Size: 10¹/₂"w x 14"h

Supplies: Worsted weight yarn, metallic cord, four 10¹/₂" x 13¹/₂" sheets of clear 7 mesh plastic canvas, #16 tapestry needle, sawtooth hanger, and craft glue

Stitches Used: Backstitch, Gobelin Stitch, Overcast Stitch, and Tent Stitch

Instructions: Follow charts to cut and stitch pieces. Using red metallic cord, join stitched Sign piece to unstitched Sign piece. Repeat for Oval pieces. Thread a 6" length of red metallic cord through Ovals and Signs at ▲'s. Tie cord into a ¹/₂" loop and trim ends. Repeat for ✱'s. Glue Angel to Oval. Glue sawtooth hanger to back of Banner.

Design by Carole L. Rodgers.

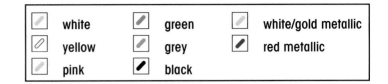

	white		green		white/gold metallic
	yellow		grey		red metallic
	pink		black		

Oval (53 x 76 threads) (cut 2, stitch 1)

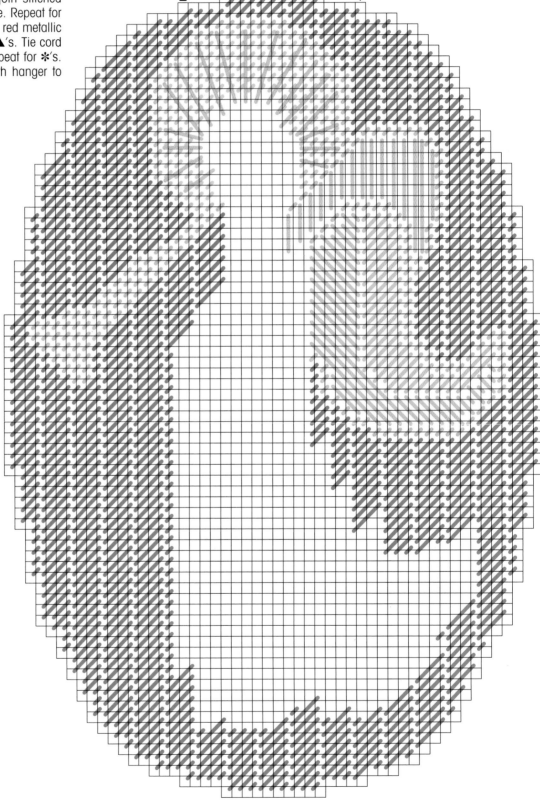

Sign (71 x 31 threads) (cut 2, stitch 1)

Angel (36 x 63 threads)

Festive Flowerpot Cover

This lovely flowerpot cover will keep the holiday spirit blooming, whether it's used as a centerpiece or presented to a friend. Glittering with gold beads and metallic yarn, the festive design is a handsome way to display Yuletide blossoms.

FESTIVE FLOWERPOT COVER

Size: 5¹/₂"h x 7" dia

Supplies: Worsted weight yarn, gold metallic braid, one 13¹/₂" x 22" sheet of clear 7 mesh plastic canvas, thirty-four 6mm gold beads, nylon line, sewing needle (for working with nylon line), 5"h x 6" dia planter, and #16 tapestry needle

Stitches Used: Gobelin Stitch, Mosaic Stitch, Overcast Stitch, and Stem Stitch

Instructions: Cut a 138 x 36 thread piece of plastic canvas. Follow chart to stitch design, repeating stitch patterns to right edge of canvas. Attach beads to stitched piece using nylon line. Using matching color yarn, join short edges of canvas together, forming a cylinder.

Design by Dick Martin.

gold metallic
red
green
gold bead

Flowerpot Cover (138 x 36 threads)

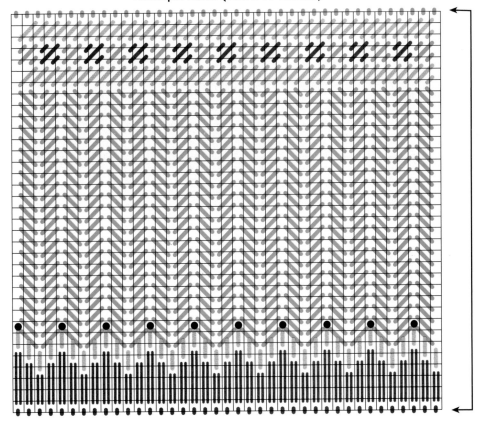

Continue stitching design to right edge of canvas

Holiday Doorknob Basket

Deck the door with a wee basket of candy, and you'll cater to everyone's sweet tooth. With a merry reminder to enjoy this special season, our crafty doorknob basket puts yummy treats right at your fingertips — and bestows holiday spirit on an often-overlooked spot.

HOLIDAY DOORKNOB BASKET

Size: 3¹/₄"w x 9¹/₄"h x 1³/₄"d

Supplies: Worsted weight yarn, embroidery floss, one 10¹/₂" x 13¹/₂" sheet of red 7 mesh plastic canvas, one 10¹/₂" x 13¹/₂" sheet of white 7 mesh plastic canvas, one 8" x 11" sheet of white 14 mesh perforated plastic, one 3" dia plastic canvas circle, #16 tapestry needle, and #24 tapestry needle

Stitches Used: Cross Stitch, Gobelin Stitch, Mosaic Stitch, Overcast Stitch, and Tent Stitch

Instructions: Refer to photo for canvas color of each piece. Follow charts to cut and stitch pieces.

Using dk green yarn, match ▲'s and *'s to join Front to Back. Follow Cutting Diagram to cut circle for Bottom. Join Bottom to Front and Back. Insert Sign under Gobelin Stitches on Back.

Design by Ann Townsend.

Cutting Diagram for Bottom

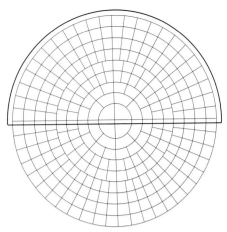

WORSTED WEIGHT YARN	
✎	dk red
✎	green
✎	dk brown
EMBROIDERY FLOSS	
✎	dk red

Front
7 mesh (34 x 18 threads)

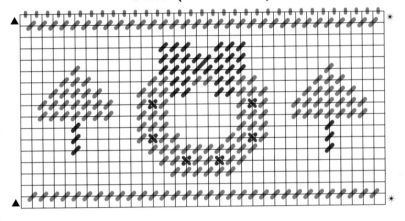

Back
7 mesh (21 x 61 threads)

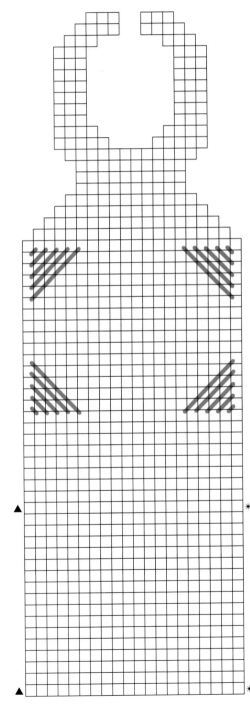

Sign
14 mesh (39 x 30 threads)

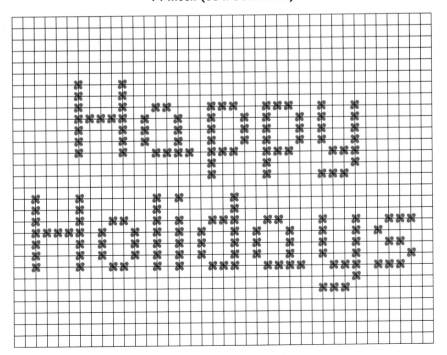

Candy Cane Collection

Add a new twist to your tree with an unbeatable team — Santa and candy canes! Cleverly fashioned into a sleigh runner, a heart frame, or just a jolly accompaniment to Kris Kringle, these versatile candy canes add color and charm to your Yuletide tree.

CANDY CANE COLLECTION

Approx Size: 4"w x 4½"h each

Supplies for One Ornament: Worsted weight yarn, one 10½" x 13½" sheet of clear 7 mesh plastic canvas, #16 tapestry needle, and nylon line

Stitches Used: Backstitch, Cross Stitch, French Knot, Gobelin Stitch, Mosaic Stitch, Overcast Stitch, and Tent Stitch

Instructions: Follow chart to cut and stitch desired Ornament. For hanger, thread 8" of nylon line through top of Ornament. Tie ends of nylon line into a knot 3" above Ornament and trim ends.

Designs by Dick Martin.

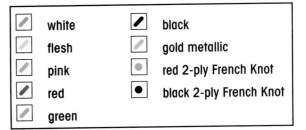

white		black	
flesh		gold metallic	
pink		red 2-ply French Knot	
red		black 2-ply French Knot	
green			

Heart (27 x 27 threads)

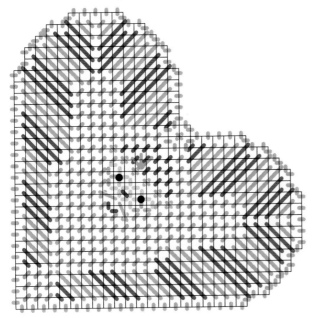

Sleigh (32 x 31 threads)

Santa Face (29 x 28 threads)

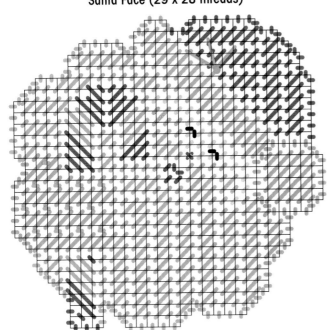

Candy Cane (32 x 31 threads)

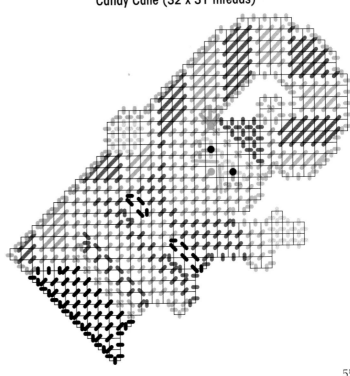

Cheery Faces

Put on a cheery holiday face with our tissue box covers and tote bag! You can make all three cover-ups for your kitchen, bedroom, and bath, or use them as gifts for a friend or two! The tote, which can be made with any of the three faces, is perfect for holiday deliveries, such as Christmas cards and little gifts.

CHEERY FACES

TOTE BAG
Approx Size: 5"w x 9½"h x 2¾"d

Supplies for One Tote Bag: Worsted weight yarn, two 10½" x 13½" sheets of white 7 mesh plastic canvas, #16 tapestry needle, and craft glue

For Santa only, one 1" white pom-pom

Stitches Used: Backstitch, French Knot, Gobelin Stitch, Mosaic Stitch, Overcast Stitch, Scotch Stitch, and Tent Stitch

Instructions: Follow chart to cut and stitch desired Front piece. If desired, omit white background stitches on face.

For Back, cut a piece of plastic canvas 32 x 38 threads. For Sides, cut two pieces of plastic canvas 18 x 38 threads each. For Handle, cut a piece of plastic canvas 6 x 75 threads. For Bottom, cut a piece of plastic canvas 32 x 18 threads. Back, Sides, Handle, and Bottom are not stitched.

Using matching color yarn, join Front to Sides. Join Back to Sides. Join Bottom to Front, Back, and Sides. Join Handle to Sides.

For Santa only, glue pom-pom to Front.

TISSUE BOX COVERS
Approx Size: 5½"w x 6¼"h x 5"d each

(**Note:** Fits a 4¼"w x 5¼"h x 4¼"d boutique tissue box.)

Supplies for One Tissue Box Cover: Worsted weight yarn, two 10½" x 13½" sheets of white 7 mesh plastic canvas, #16 tapestry needle, and craft glue

For Santa only, one 1" white pom-pom

Stitches Used: Backstitch, French Knot, Gobelin Stitch, Mosaic Stitch, Overcast Stitch, Scotch Stitch, and Tent Stitch

Instructions: Follow chart to cut and stitch desired Front piece. Cut and stitch Top, Side, and Back pieces.

Using yarn color to match Front, join Front to Sides. Using red yarn, join Sides to Back. Join Top to Side and Back pieces. Tack Top to Front. Using matching color yarn, cover remaining unworked edges of Tissue Box Cover.

For Santa only, glue pom-pom to Front.

Designs by Ann Townsend.

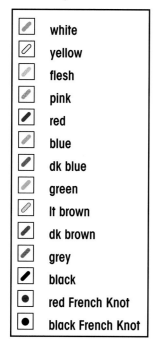

▨	white
▨	yellow
▨	flesh
▨	pink
▨	red
▨	blue
▨	dk blue
▨	green
▨	lt brown
▨	dk brown
▨	grey
▨	black
●	red French Knot
●	black French Knot

Snowman Front (36 x 43 threads)

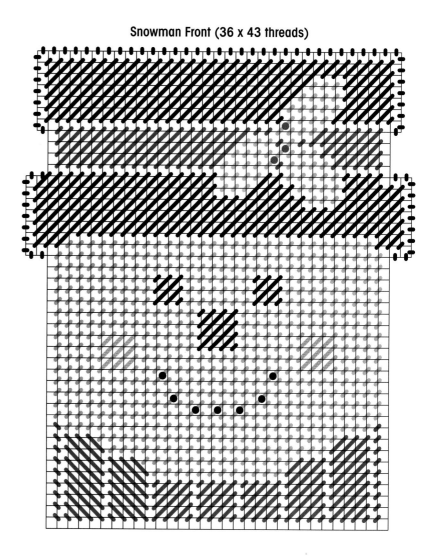

Santa Front (43 x 46 threads)

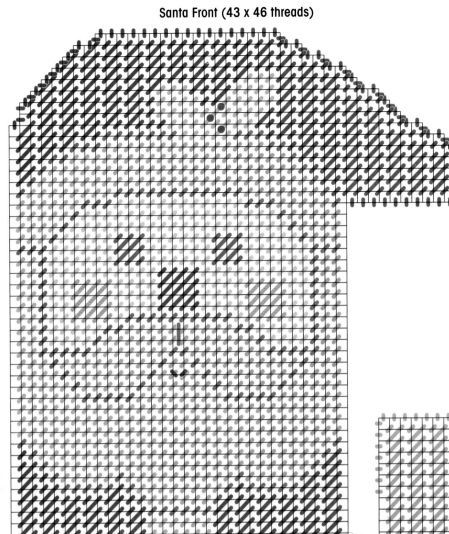

Soldier Front (32 x 45 threads)

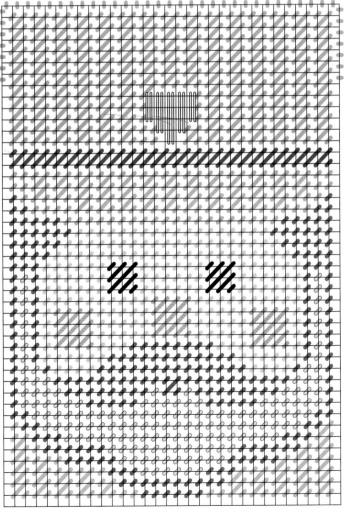

Continued on page 60

Tissue Box Cover Top (32 x 32 threads)

	white
	red
	green

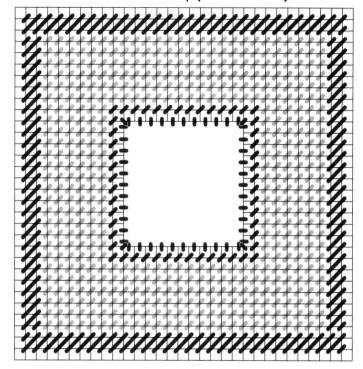

Tissue Box Cover Side/Back

(32 x 38 threads) (stitch 3)

Christmas Night Door Pillow

Our lovely hanging pillow, worked on 10 mesh canvas, is a handsome reminder of Clement Clarke Moore's beloved Christmas poem. Hung on a bedroom door, it ensures visions of sugarplums and a good night to all. This beautiful silhouette of Santa's reindeer and sleigh flying away "like the down of a thistle" will heighten the holiday excitement in your household.

CHRISTMAS NIGHT DOOR PILLOW

Size: 10¼"w x 12"h x 1¼"d

Supplies: Sport weight yarn, dk red embroidery floss, one 10½" x 13½" sheet of clear 10 mesh plastic canvas, two yds of ⅜"w dk red twisted cording, #20 tapestry needle, nylon line, polyester fiberfill, and craft glue

Stitches Used: Backstitch, Cross Stitch, Overcast Stitch, and Tent Stitch

Instructions: Follow chart to cut and stitch design. Before adding Backstitches, complete background with ecru Tent Stitches as noted on chart. For Back, cut a 98 x 65 thread piece of plastic canvas. Back is not stitched.

Using ecru yarn, join Front to Back, leaving a small opening to insert polyester fiberfill. Lightly stuff pillow. Join remaining unworked edges together.

Using nylon line, tack cording to edges of pillow. Cut cording desired length for hanger. Glue hanger to back of pillow.

Design by Deborah Lambein.

Chart note: This chart represents one 98 x 65 thread canvas piece. It is spread across two pages to make it large enough to be followed easily. No threads or stitches are repeated from one page to the next.

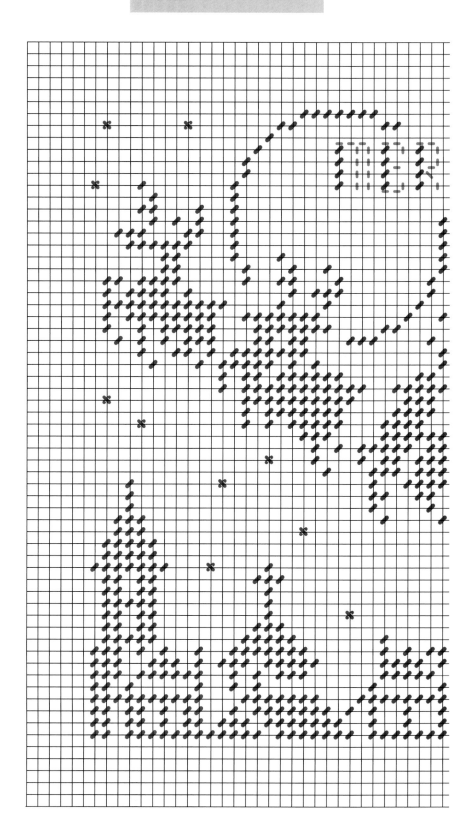

✎	ecru
✎	dk red
✎	dk red floss - 3 strands

Pillow Front (98 x 65 threads)

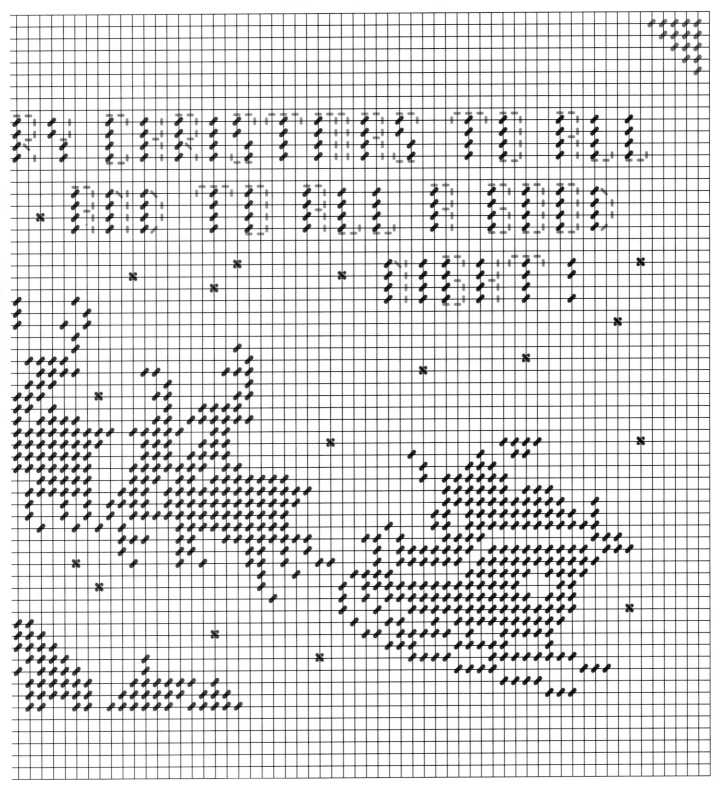

Candlestick Angel Choir

A choir of candlestick angels displayed in beautiful brass holders makes a stunning holiday centerpiece. Decorated with gold chenille-stem halos and gilded stars, our lofty seraphim bring a touch of heaven to your Yuletide decor.

CANDLESTICK ANGEL CHOIR

Size: 3"w x 11 1/4"h x 1 3/4"d

Supplies for One Candlestick: Worsted weight yarn, one 10 1/2" x 13 1/2" sheet of clear 7 mesh soft plastic canvas, #16 tapestry needle, 1" wooden star, gold metallic paint (optional), 6" length of gold metallic thread, and one gold metallic chenille stem

Stitches Used: Backstitch, French Knot, Gobelin Stitch, Overcast Stitch, and Tent Stitch

Instructions: Follow charts to cut and stitch pieces. Using matching color yarn, cover unworked edges of Arms and Wings. Join Angel together along long edges to form a cylinder. Matching ★'s and ♦'s, tack Arms to Angel using white yarn. Matching ■'s, securely tack Wings to Angel.

To form halo, wrap one end of chenille stem around top of Angel. Twist chenille stem together to secure. Shape remaining end of chenille stem into a circle 3/4" above Angel. Twist chenille stem together to secure and trim ends.

If desired, paint star. Run gold metallic thread under stitches on hands. Glue ends of thread to back of star.

Design by Becky Dill.

⟋	white
⟋	flesh
⟋	rose
⟋	tan
●	white French Knot
●	blue French Knot

Angel
(16 x 70 threads)

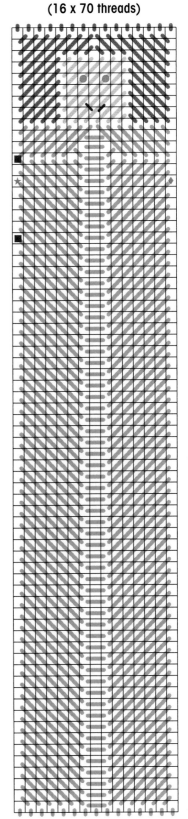

Wings
(20 x 45 threads)

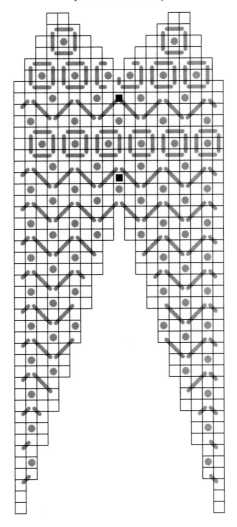

Arms

(40 x 4 threads)

Snowy Cottage Doorstop

Introduce the holiday spirit right at your front doorstep with a Yuletide scene pretty enough to grace a greeting card! With its snow-trimmed landscape and cozy cottage, this unique doorstop is a charming way to share Christmas greetings with friends and family.

SNOWY COTTAGE DOORSTOP

Size: 8¼"w x 5¾"h x 2¾"d

Supplies: Worsted weight yarn, white embroidery floss, two 10½" x 13½" sheets of clear 7 mesh plastic canvas, 7½"w x 3½"h x 2⅛"d brick, plastic wrap, and #16 tapestry needle

Stitches Used: Backstitch, French Knot, Gobelin Stitch, Modified Couching Stitch, Overcast Stitch, Tent Stitch, and Turkey Loop Stitch

Instructions: Follow charts to cut and stitch pieces. For Top and Bottom, cut two pieces of plastic canvas 54 x 16 threads each. For Back, cut a piece of plastic canvas 54 x 27 threads. Cover Top and Back with lt blue Tent Stitches. Bottom is not stitched.

With wrong sides facing inward, join Front to Sides using matching color yarn. Using blue yarn, join Top to Front along unworked edges of Front. Tack Top securely in place. Using matching color yarn, join Sides to Back. Wrap brick with plastic wrap and insert brick into Doorstop. Using matching color yarn, join Bottom to Front, Back, and Sides.

Design by Joyce Levitt.

EMBROIDERY FLOSS	
✎	white - 1 strand

YARN	
✎	white
✎	red
✎	lt blue
✎	blue
✎	lt green
✎	green
✎	black 2-ply
●	white French Knot
●	lt green French Knot
●	green French Knot
●	black French Knot
○	white Turkey Loop
○	lt green Turkey Loop

Side A
(16 x 27 threads)

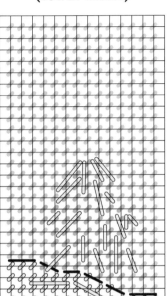

Side B
(16 x 27 threads)

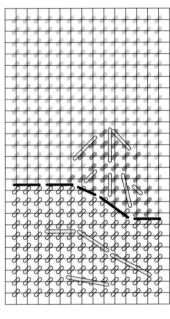

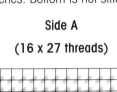

Front (54 x 38 threads)

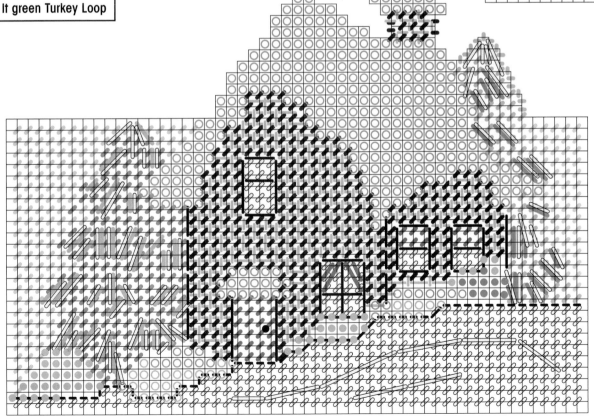

67

Windswept Snowman

Our whimsical snowman stands ready to brave winter's chills (and warm your heart!). This eye-catching centerpiece, with its miniature red forest, has imaginative finishing touches — a windswept scarf, coal-button eyes, and puffy mittens and buttons.

WINDSWEPT SNOWMAN

Snowman Size: $10^3/4$"w x $11^1/4$"h x $6^1/2$"d
Large Tree Size: 6"w x $10^3/4$"h x $3^3/4$"d
Medium Tree Size: $4^3/4$"w x 7"h x $3^1/4$"d
Small Tree Size: $3^3/4$"w x $5^1/4$"h x $3^3/4$"d
Supplies: Worsted weight yarn, five $10^1/2$" x $13^1/2$" sheets of white 7 mesh plastic canvas, #16 tapestry needle, five $1^1/2$" white pom-poms, 9mm white chenille stem, and polyester fiberfill
Stitches Used: Backstitch, Fringe Stitch, Gobelin Stitch, Mosaic Stitch, Overcast Stitch, Scotch Stitch, and Tent Stitch
Instructions: Follow charts to cut pieces. **Working through two thicknesses** of plastic canvas, stitch Snowman Base, Large Tree Base, Medium Tree Base, and Small Tree Base. Follow charts to stitch remaining pieces, leaving stitches in shaded areas unworked.

Matching ★'s and ◆'s, join Large Tree pieces to Large Tree Base using white yarn. Using red yarn, join Large Tree pieces together along unworked edges. Repeat for Medium and Small Tree pieces.

Using red yarn, tack Nose to Snowman. Using matching color yarn, match ♥'s and join Scarf to Snowman. Using white yarn, tack pom-poms to Snowman.

Matching ✳'s and ❖'s, join Snowman pieces to Snowman Base using white yarn. Using matching color yarn, join Snowman pieces together along unworked edges while lightly stuffing with polyester fiberfill. Work Fringe Stitches in shaded area through both thickness of plastic canvas.

Wrap chenille stem twice around hat on Snowman. Using white yarn, tack Candy Cane to Snowman. Trim Fringe on Snowman to 1" long.

Design by Dick Martin.

Candy Cane
(16 x 42 threads)

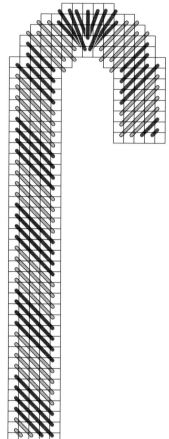

Snowman Base (44 x 44 threads) (cut 2)

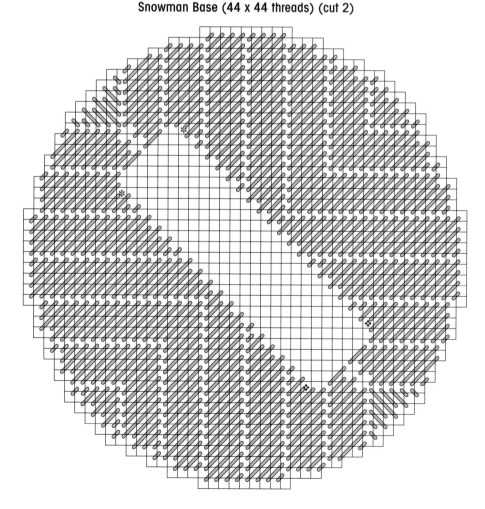

Small Tree (24 x 35 threads) (stitch 2)

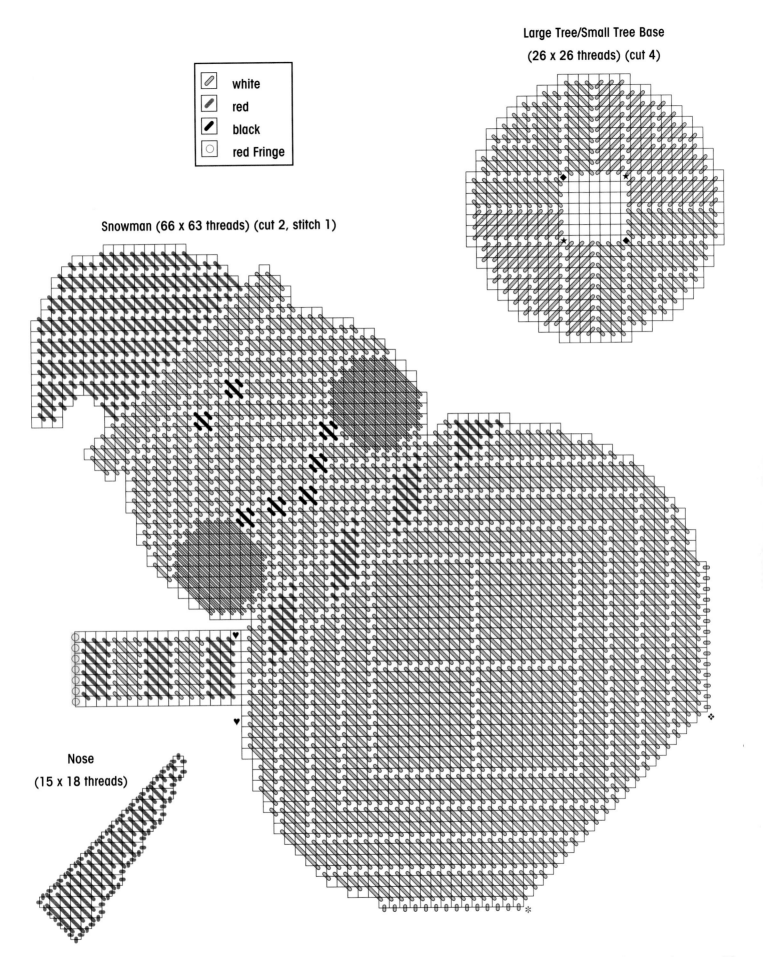

Large Tree/Small Tree Base
(26 x 26 threads) (cut 4)

white
red
black
red Fringe

Snowman (66 x 63 threads) (cut 2, stitch 1)

Nose
(15 x 18 threads)

Continued on page 72

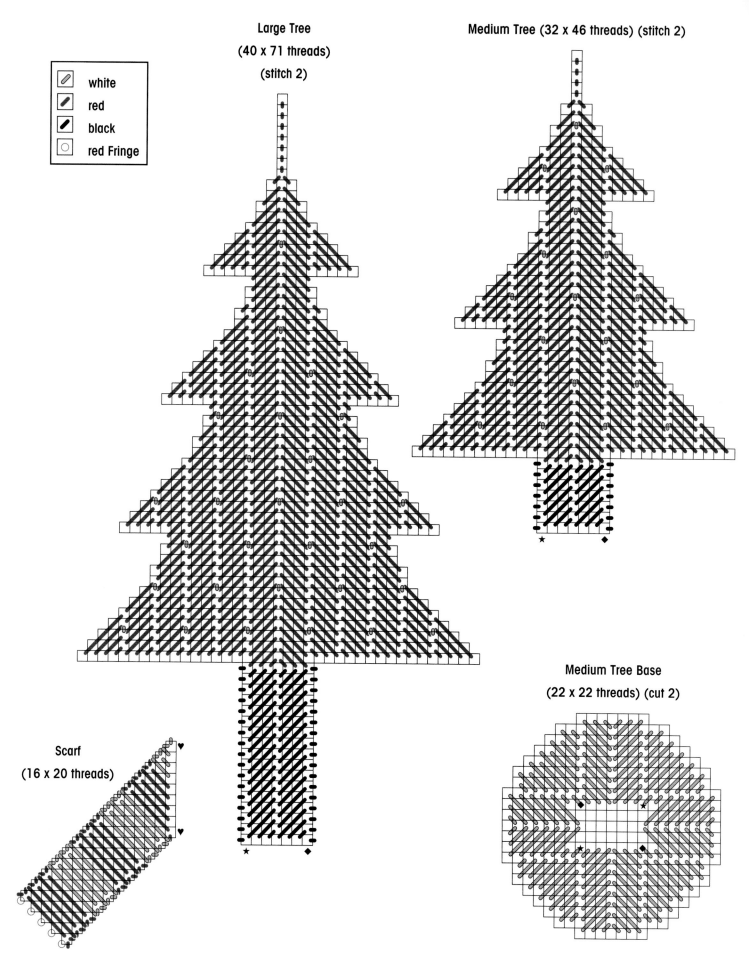

Large Tree
(40 x 71 threads)
(stitch 2)

Medium Tree (32 x 46 threads) (stitch 2)

white
red
black
red Fringe

Medium Tree Base
(22 x 22 threads) (cut 2)

Scarf
(16 x 20 threads)

Perky Package Coasters

A sprinkling of white French knots creates a perky polka dot pattern on four Christmas "gift" coasters. With a matching stand-up holder, these coasters are an eye-catching accent even when not in use!

PERKY PACKAGE COASTERS

Coaster Size: 3¼"w x 4"h
Box Size: 4"w x 2"h x 1"d
Supplies: Worsted weight yarn, one 10½" x 13½" sheet of clear 7 mesh plastic canvas, and #16 tapestry needle
Stitches Used: Backstitch, French Knot, Gobelin Stitch, Overcast Stitch, and Tent Stitch
Instructions: Follow charts to cut and stitch pieces. Cut a 26 x 7 thread piece of plastic canvas for Box Bottom. Bottom is not stitched. Using matching color yarn, join Box Front to Sides. Join Back to Sides. Join Bottom to Front, Back, and Sides.

Design by Joan Green.

╱	red
╱	dk red
╱	green
●	white 2-ply French Knot

Box Side
(7 x 13 threads) (stitch 2)

Coaster
(22 x 26 threads) (stitch 4)

Box Front/Back

(26 x 13 threads) (stitch 2)

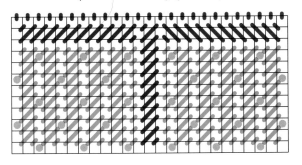

Photo Frame Train

Track down your favorite photos of memorable holiday moments with this clever photo frame train. Whether it's displayed at the office, home, or Grandma's house, this frame set will keep your precious cargo in clear sight — no matter what your schedule!

PHOTO FRAME TRAIN

Size: 13¼"w x 3½"h
(Each photo opening is approx 1¼"w x 1¼"h.)

Supplies: Worsted weight yarn, one 10½" x 13½" sheet of clear 7 mesh plastic canvas, #16 tapestry needle, and craft glue

Stitches Used: French Knot, Overcast Stitch, and Tent Stitch

Instructions: Follow charts to cut and stitch pieces. Glue photos to wrong sides of Front pieces. For each Back, cut another Front piece from plastic canvas, omitting the photo opening. Referring to photo for yarn colors, join Front pieces to Back pieces. Using matching color yarn, tack Engine, Cars, and Caboose together.

Design by Maryanne Moreck.

⟋	lt gold
⟋	gold
⟋	pink
⟋	red
⟋	green
⟋	dk green
⟋	black
•	white French Knot

Engine Front (36 x 24 threads)

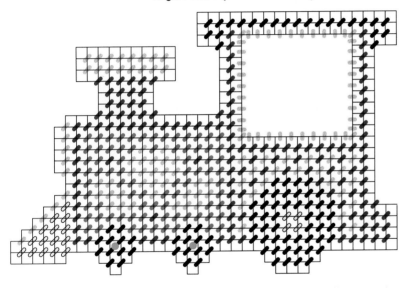

Car #1 Front (17 x 22 threads)

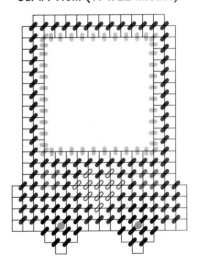

Car #2 Front (17 x 22 threads)

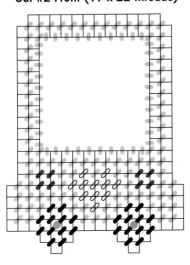

Caboose Front (20 x 22 threads)

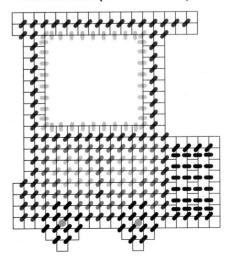

Snowflake Jar Lids

Put a frosty touch on holiday treats with our trio of wintry containers. You can pack the wide-mouth jars with candies or a little something special for a favorite friend. The lacy pearl-embellished snowflakes on the lids are stitched on red, green, and blue 10 mesh canvas.

SNOWFLAKE JAR LIDS

Size: 3¼" dia each

Supplies for One Jar Lid: Sport weight yarn, one 10½" x 13½" sheet of desired color 10 mesh plastic canvas, 3mm pearl beads, wide-mouth jar lid ring (3" dia opening), #20 tapestry needle, nylon line, sewing needle (for working with nylon line), and craft glue

Stitch Used: Cross Stitch

Instructions: Follow charts to cut and stitch desired Snowflake design. Attach beads to stitched piece using nylon line. Glue stitched piece to jar lid ring.

Designs by Kandace Thomas.

	white
	pearl bead

Snowflake #1
(32 x 32 threads)

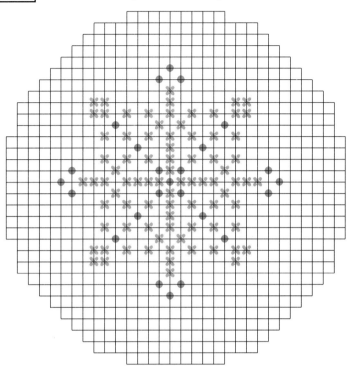

Snowflake #2
(32 x 32 threads)

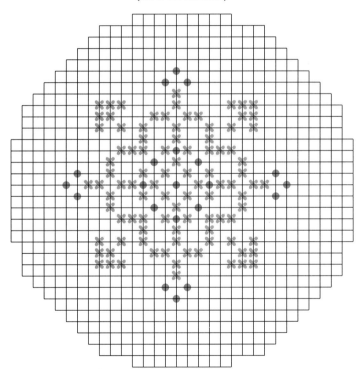

Snowflake #3
(32 x 32 threads)

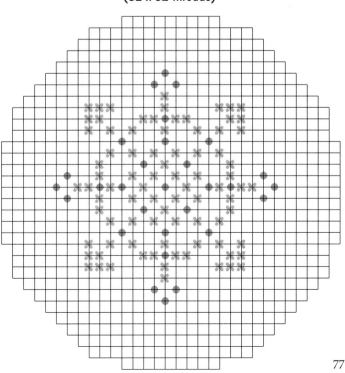

WINTRY NIGHT FRAME

This one-of-a-kind frame surrounds a loved one with a winter woodland scene. A crescent moon, twinkling stars, and a cabin nestled in a mountain glade make a rustic backdrop for a fireside photo or a snapshot of frisky outdoor activities — from building snowmen to making snow angels!

WINTRY NIGHT FRAME

Size: 10¼"w x 8¼"h x 2¼"d
(Photo opening is 4¾"w x 2¾"h.)

Supplies: Worsted weight yarn, two 10½" x 13½" sheets of white 7 mesh plastic canvas, #16 tapestry needle, and craft glue

Stitches Used: Cross Stitch, Tent Stitch, and Overcast Stitch

Instructions: Follow chart to cut and stitch Frame Front. Glue picture to back of Frame Front. For Frame Back, cut a 69 x 55 thread piece of plastic canvas. For Frame Base, cut a 69 x 15 piece of plastic canvas. Back and Base are not stitched.

Using red yarn, join top edge of Frame Front to one long edge of Frame Back. Join bottom edge of Frame Front to one long edge of Base. Join remaining long edges of Base and Frame Back together.

Design by Polly Carbonari.

⊘ yellow		⊘ dk green	
⊘ red		⊘ tan	
⊘ rust		⊘ brown	
⊘ blue		⊘ black	
⊘ green			

Frame Front (69 x 55 threads)

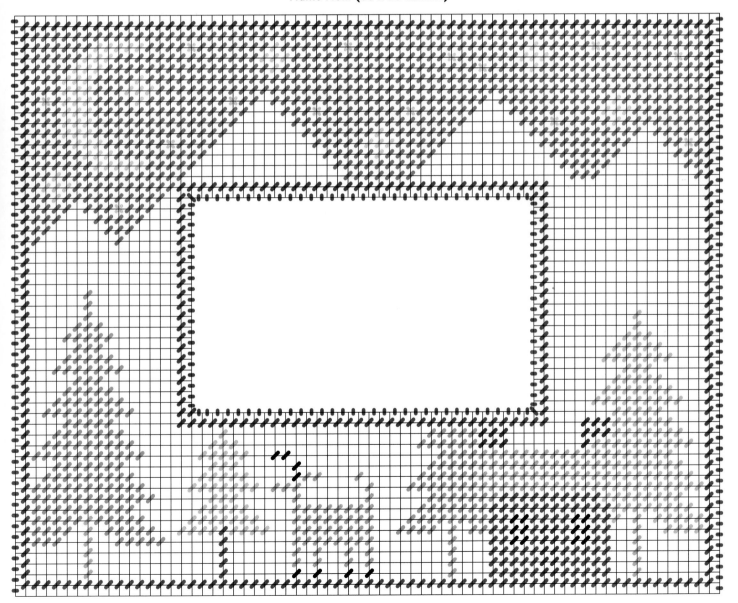

Christmas Sitters

Go out on a limb with our Christmas sitters! You can also display them on a mantel, windowsill, or country shelf — anywhere you want to add a merry touch. With their colorful costumes and cheerful faces, these holiday buddies will perk up any nook or cranny.

CHRISTMAS SITTERS

Supplies: Worsted weight yarn, two 10¹/₂" x 13¹/₂" sheets of 7 mesh plastic canvas, #16 tapestry needle, seven ³/₈" gold jingle bells, and sewing needle and thread

Stitches Used: Backstitch, Cross Stitch, French Knot, Gobelin Stitch, Overcast Stitch, Tent Stitch, and Turkey Loop Stitch

REINDEER

Size: 3"w x 11"h x 1³/₄"d

Instructions: Follow charts to cut and stitch Reindeer pieces. Using sewing needle and thread, tack jingle bells to Body.

Cut thirty-six 12" lengths of tan yarn. Place nine lengths together and tie a knot close to one end. With knot on back of Body, thread loose ends through one opening in upper Body. To form elbow, tie a knot 1" from Body. Tie a third knot 1³/₄" from elbow and trim ends. Refer to photo to place third knot between one Glove A and one Glove B. Using matching color yarn, join Glove pieces together along unworked edges. Repeat for remaining upper opening and Glove pieces.

Place nine lengths of tan yarn together and tie a knot close to one end. With knot on back of Body, thread loose ends through one opening in lower Body. To form knee, tie a knot 2" from Body. Tie a third knot 2¹/₂" from knee and trim ends. Refer to photo to place third knot between two Boot pieces. Using matching color yarn, join Boot pieces together along unworked edges. Repeat for remaining lower opening and Boot pieces.

Using matching color yarn, match ▲'s and join ends of Body together. Using tan yarn, join Bottom to Body.

Designs by Linda Huffman.

✏	white
✏	red
✏	tan
✏	brown
✏	brown 2-ply
●	red French Knot
●	black French Knot

Reindeer Boot

(10 x 12 threads)

(stitch 4)

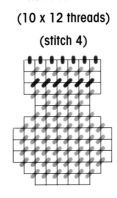

Reindeer Glove A

(7 x 9 threads)

(stitch 2)

Reindeer Glove B

(7 x 9 threads)

(stitch 2)

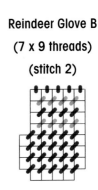

Reindeer Body (37 x 37 threads)

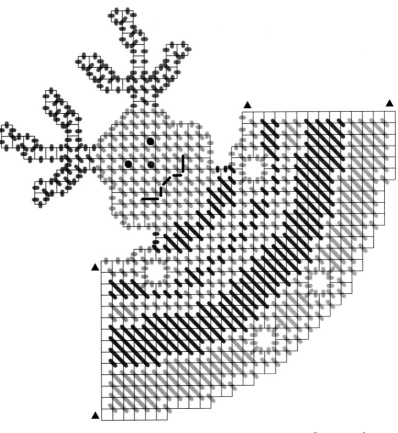

Reindeer Bottom

(16 x 11 threads)

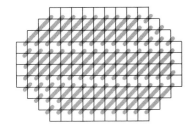

Continued on page 82

SANTA

Size: 2½"w x 10½"h x 1¾"d

Instructions: Follow charts to cut and stitch Santa pieces. Using sewing needle and thread, tack jingle bells to Body and Boot pieces.

Cut thirty-six 12" lengths of red yarn. Place nine lengths together and tie a knot close to one end. With knot on back of Body, thread loose ends through one opening in upper Body. To form elbow, tie a knot 1" from Body. Tie a third knot 1¾" from elbow and trim ends. Refer to photo to place third knot between one Glove A and one Glove B. Using matching color yarn, join Glove pieces together along unworked edges. Repeat for remaining upper opening and Glove pieces.

Place nine lengths of red yarn together and tie a knot close to one end. With knot on back of Body, thread loose ends through one opening in lower Body. To form knee, tie a knot 2" from Body. Tie a third knot 2½" from knee and trim ends. Refer to photo to place third knot between two Boot pieces. Using black yarn, join Boot pieces together along unworked edges. Repeat for remaining lower opening and Boot pieces.

Using matching color yarn, match ▲'s and join ends of Body together. Using white yarn, join Bottom to Body.

⬈	white
⬈	flesh
⬈	gold
⬈	red
⬈	black
⬤	red French Knot
⬤	black French Knot
◯	white Turkey Loop

Santa Boot
(8 x 10 threads)
(stitch 4)

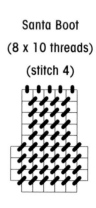

Santa Glove A
(7 x 8 threads)
(stitch 2)

Santa Glove B
(7 x 8 threads)
(stitch 2)

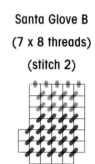

Santa Bottom
(16 x 11 threads)

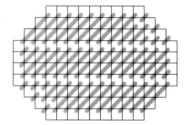

Santa Body (31 x 32 threads)

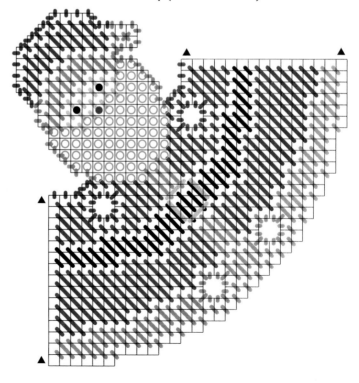

82

SOLDIER

Size: 2³/₄"w x 10¹/₄"h x 1³/₄"d

Instructions: Follow charts to cut and stitch Soldier pieces.

Cut eighteen 12" lengths of red yarn and eighteen 12" lengths of blue yarn. Place nine lengths of red yarn together and tie a knot close to one end. With knot on back of Body, thread loose ends through one opening in upper Body. To form elbow, tie a knot 1" from Body. Tie a third knot 1³/₄" from elbow and trim ends. Refer to photo to place third knot between one Glove A and one Glove B. Using matching color yarn, join Glove pieces together along unworked edges. Repeat for remaining upper opening and Glove pieces.

Place nine lengths of blue yarn together and tie a knot close to one end. With knot on back of Body, thread loose ends through one opening in lower Body. To form knee, tie a knot 2" from Body. Tie a third knot 2¹/₂" from knee and trim ends. Refer to photo to place third knot between one Boot Front and one Boot Back. Using black yarn, join Boot pieces together along unworked edges. Repeat for remaining lower opening and Boot pieces.

Using matching color yarn, match ▲'s and join ends of Body together. Using blue yarn, join Bottom to Body. Using black yarn, tack Rifle to Body.

▨	flesh
▨	gold
▨	gold 2-ply
◪	red
◪	red 2-ply
▨	blue
◪	brown
◼	black
▨	black 2-ply
⬤	gold French Knot
⬤	black French Knot

Soldier Rifle

(5 x 27 threads)

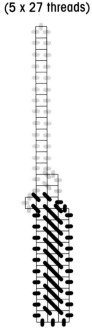

Soldier Bottom

(16 x 11 threads)

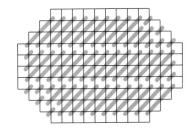

Soldier Glove B

(8 x 9 threads)

(stitch 2)

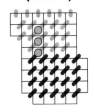

Soldier Glove A

(8 x 9 threads)

(stitch 2)

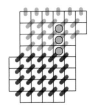

Soldier Boot Front

(10 x 14 threads)

(stitch 2)

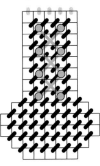

Soldier Boot Back

(10 x 14 threads)

(stitch 2)

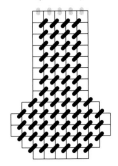

Soldier Body (32 x 32 threads)

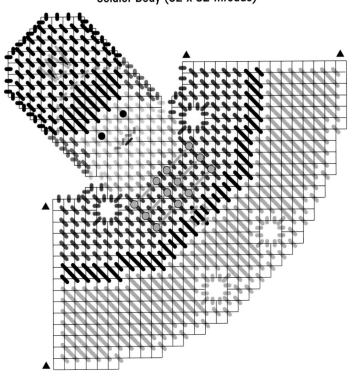

Penguin Cart

Three precious penguins, worked on 10 mesh canvas and harnessed with a bright red ribbon, pull a colorful cart designed to hold delicious Yuletide treats. Fresh from the South Pole, this irresistible trio of fine feathered friends and their versatile wagon make an eye-catching holiday accent!

PENGUIN CART

Cart Size: 6"w x 4¼"h x 3¾"d
Penguin Size: 2½"w x 3½"h x 1"d

Supplies: Worsted weight yarn, sport weight yarn, two 10½" x 13½" sheets of clear 7 mesh plastic canvas, one 10½" x 13½" sheet of clear 10 mesh plastic canvas, #16 tapestry needle, #20 tapestry needle, two yds of ¼"w red satin ribbon, and craft glue

Stitches Used: Backstitch, French Knot, Gobelin Stitch, Overcast Stitch, and Tent Stitch

Instructions: Follow charts to cut and stitch pieces. For Cart Side, stitch through two thicknesses of plastic canvas to make two Side pieces. For Cart Front/Back, stitch through two thicknesses of plastic canvas to make one Front piece and one Back piece. For Penguin Feet, stitch through two thicknesses of plastic canvas to make three Feet pieces. Using black yarn, cover unworked edges of Penguin Arm pieces.

Using matching color yarn, join one Cart Side to Front. Repeat for remaining Side. Join Sides to Back. Using white yarn, stack Bottom pieces and join to Front, Sides, and Back through all thicknesses of plastic canvas.

Weave ribbon over and under sets of two Gobelin Stitches at top and bottom of Cart as shown in photo. Glue ends of ribbon to Cart to secure. Tie a 16" length of ribbon into a bow and trim ends. Glue bow to Front.

Using black yarn, match ■'s and tack Arm A to Penguin Front. Matching ★'s, tack Arm B to Penguin Back. Using matching color yarn, join Penguin Front to Back, leaving area between ▲'s and ✳'s unworked. Using gold yarn, match ▲'s and ✳'s to join Penguin to Feet through all thicknesses of plastic canvas. Using gold yarn, cover unworked edges of Feet. Repeat for remaining Penguin pieces.

Using black yarn, join two Wheel pieces together. Repeat for remaining Wheels. Glue Wheels to Cart. Using desired length of red ribbon, glue one end of ribbon to Cart Front and string Penguins in a row, threading ribbon through each Penguin Front and gluing loose end of ribbon to last Penguin Back.

Design by Jack Peatman for LuvLee Designs.

Wheel (12 x 12 threads)

(stitch 8) 7 mesh

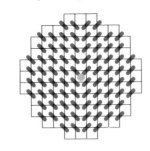

Cart Front/Back (25 x 23 threads)

(cut 4) 7 mesh

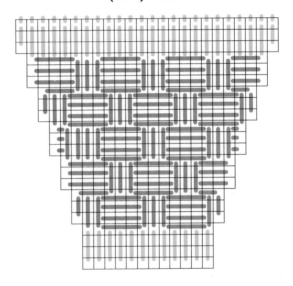

Cart Side (41 x 23 threads)

(cut 4) 7 mesh

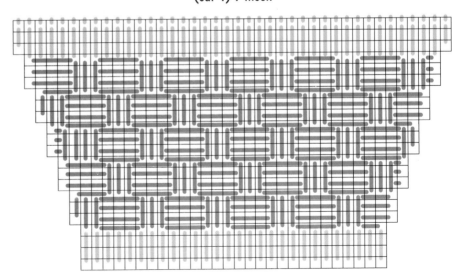

Continued on page 86

SPORT WEIGHT YARN

- white
- gold
- green - 2 strands
- black
- red French Knot
- blue French Knot

Cart Bottom (29 x 13 threads)

(cut 2) 7 mesh

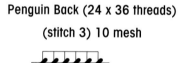

Penguin Arm A

(7 x 12 threads)

(stitch 3) 10 mesh

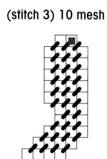

Penguin Arm B

(7 x 12 threads)

(stitch 3) 10 mesh

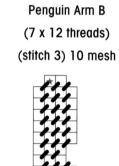

Penguin Feet

(10 x 12 threads)

(cut 6) 10 mesh

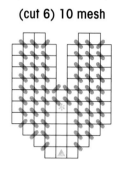

Penguin Front (24 x 36 threads)

(stitch 3) 10 mesh

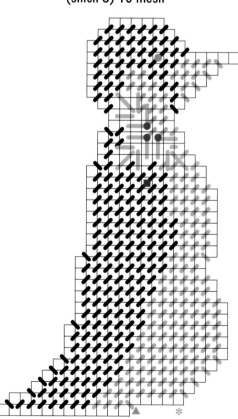

Penguin Back (24 x 36 threads)

(stitch 3) 10 mesh

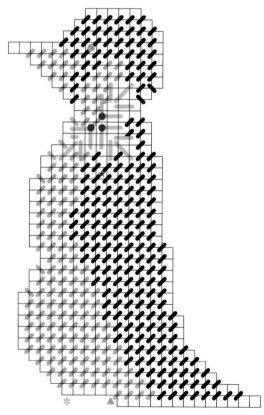

PEPPERMINT GIFT BAG SET

Bright tissue paper shines through these simple gift bags decorated with bells or a lovable teddy. Diagonal overcast stitches of red and white yarn join the sections with a candy-cane effect. Use the jingling "Noel" clip to top off a festive bag, or tuck it inside its matching tote as a thoughtful gift.

PEPPERMINT GIFT BAG SET
NOEL TOTE BAG
Size: 4$\frac{1}{2}$"w x 8$\frac{1}{2}$"h x 2$\frac{1}{2}$"d
Supplies: Worsted weight yarn, one 10$\frac{1}{2}$" x 13$\frac{1}{2}$" sheet of white 7 mesh plastic canvas, #16 tapestry needle, and four $\frac{1}{2}$" gold jingle bells
Stitches Used: Alternating Overcast Stitch, Backstitch, Cross Stitch, French Knot, Lazy Daisy Stitch, Overcast Stitch, and Tent Stitch
Instructions: Follow charts to cut and stitch pieces. For Back, cut a 30 x 36 thread piece of plastic canvas. Back is not stitched.
Using red and white Alternating Overcast Stitches, join Sides to Back. Join Bottom to Sides and Back.
Using red yarn, tie bells to Front at ▲'s. Using Alternating Overcast Stitches and Overcast Stitches, refer to photo for yarn color and join Front to Sides and Bottom.
Using red and white Alternating Overcast Stitches, cover unworked edges of pieces. Matching ✳'s, tack Handle to Tote Bag.

Design by Diane W. Villano.

NOEL BAG CLIP
Size: 4$\frac{1}{2}$"w x 2$\frac{1}{2}$"h
Supplies: Worsted weight yarn, one 10$\frac{1}{2}$" x 13$\frac{1}{2}$" sheet of white 7 mesh plastic canvas, #16 tapestry needle, four $\frac{1}{2}$" gold jingle bells, 1$\frac{3}{4}$" wood clothespin, paint (optional), and craft glue
Stitches Used: Cross Stitch, French Knot, Lazy Daisy Stitch, Overcast Stitch, and Tent Stitch
Instructions: Follow chart to cut and stitch Bag Clip. Using red yarn, tie jingle bells to Bag Clip at ▲'s. If desired, paint clothespin. Glue clothespin to back of Bag Clip.

Design by Diane W. Villano.

BEAR TOTE BAG
Size: 4$\frac{3}{4}$"w x 8$\frac{1}{2}$"h x 2$\frac{1}{2}$"d
Supplies: Worsted weight yarn, one 10$\frac{1}{2}$" x 13$\frac{1}{2}$" sheet of white 7 mesh plastic canvas, #16 tapestry needle, two 8mm moving eyes, 7mm black pom-pom, 12" length of $\frac{1}{4}$"w green ribbon, and craft glue
Stitches Used: Alternating Overcast Stitch, Cross Stitch, Overcast Stitch, and Tent Stitch
Instructions: Follow charts to cut and stitch pieces. For Back, cut a 31 x 36 thread piece of plastic canvas. Back is not stitched.
Using matching color Overcast Stitches, cover unworked edges of Muzzle, Heart, and Arms. Glue Muzzle, Heart, and Arms to Front. Glue moving eyes and pom-pom to Front.
Using red and white Alternating Overcast Stitches, join Front to Sides. Join Sides to Back. Join Bottom to Front, Sides, and Back. Cover unworked edges of pieces. Matching ✳'s, tack Handle to Tote Bag.

Design by Sandy and Honey for Studio M.

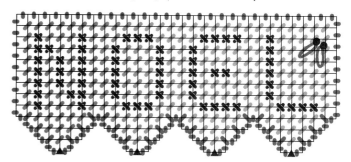

⟋	white
⟋	red
⟋	green
⟋	brown
●	red 2-ply French Knot
⟋	green 2-ply Lazy Daisy

Noel Tote Bag Front (30 x 36 threads)

Noel Bag Clip (30 x 13 threads)

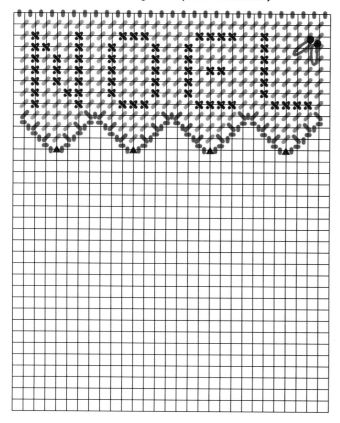

Tote Bag Handle (6 x 59 threads)

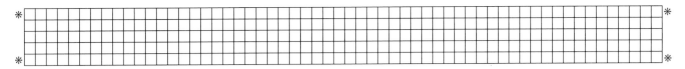

Bear Tote Bag Front (31 x 36 threads)

Tote Bag Side
(16 x 36 threads) (cut 2)

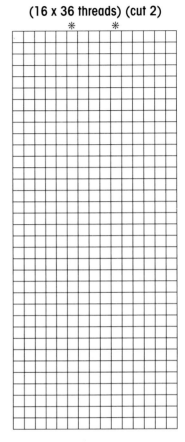

Bear Muzzle
(6 x 5 threads)

Bear Right Arm
(6 x 9 threads)

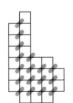

Bear Left Arm
(6 x 9 threads)

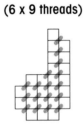

Bear Heart
(10 x 9 threads)

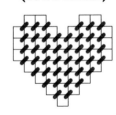

Tote Bag Bottom (30 x 16 threads)

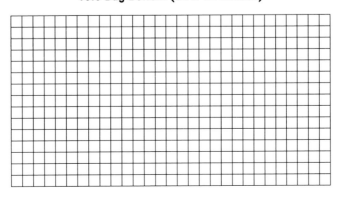

GENERAL INSTRUCTIONS
SELECTING PLASTIC CANVAS

Plastic canvas is a molded, nonwoven canvas made from clear or colored plastic. The canvas consists of "threads" and "holes." The threads aren't actually "threads" since the canvas is nonwoven, but it seems to be an accurate description of the straight lines of the canvas. The holes, as you would expect, are the spaces between the threads. The threads are often referred to in the project instructions, especially when cutting out plastic canvas pieces. The instructions for stitches will always refer to holes when explaining where to place your needle to make a stitch.

Types of Canvas. The main difference between types of plastic canvas is the mesh size. Mesh size refers to the number of holes in one inch of canvas. The most common mesh sizes are 5 mesh, 7 mesh, 10 mesh, and 14 mesh. Five mesh means that there are 5 holes in every inch of canvas. Likewise, there are 7 holes in every inch of 7 mesh canvas, 10 holes in every inch of 10 mesh canvas, and 14 holes in every inch of 14 mesh canvas. Seven mesh canvas is the most popular size for the majority of projects.

Your project supply list will tell you what size mesh you need to buy. Be sure to use the mesh size the project instructions recommend. If your project calls for 7 mesh canvas and you use 10 mesh, your finished project will be much smaller than expected. For example, suppose your instructions tell you to use 7 mesh canvas to make a boutique tissue box cover. You will need to cut each side 30 x 38 threads so they will measure $4^{1}/_{2}$" x $5^{3}/_{4}$" each. But if you were using 10 mesh canvas your sides would only measure 3" x $3^{7}/_{8}$"! Needless to say, your tissue box cover from 10 mesh canvas would not fit a boutique tissue box.

Most plastic canvas is made from clear plastic, but colored canvas is also available. Colored plastic is ideal when you don't want to stitch the entire background.

When buying canvas, you may find that some canvas is firm and rigid, while other canvas is softer and more pliable. To decide which type of canvas is right for your project, think of how the project will be used. If you are making a box or container, you will want to use firmer canvas so that the box will be sturdy and not buckle after handling. If you are making a tissue box cover, you will not need the firmer canvas because the tissue box will support the canvas and prevent warping. Softer canvas is better for projects that require a piece of canvas to be bent before it is joined to another piece.

Amount of Canvas. The project supply list usually tells you how much canvas you will need to complete the project. When buying your canvas, remember that several different manufacturers produce plastic canvas. Therefore, there are often slight variations in canvas, such as different thicknesses of threads or a small difference in mesh size. Because of these variations, try to buy enough canvas for your entire project at the same time and place. As a general rule, it is always better to buy too much canvas and have leftovers than to run out of canvas before you finish your project. By buying a little extra canvas, you not only allow for mistakes, but have extra canvas for practicing your stitches. Scraps of canvas are also excellent for making magnets and other small projects.

SELECTING YARN

You're probably thinking, "How do I select my yarn from the thousands of choices available?" Well, we have a few hints to help you choose the perfect yarns for your project and your budget.

Yarn Weight. We used various brands of worsted weight and sport weight yarn to stitch the photography models for this book. You may wish to use Needloft® Plastic Canvas Yarn in place of the worsted weight yarn. Needloft yarn is suitable only for 7 mesh plastic canvas. Refer to Types of Yarn, page 91, for additional information.

Yarn Cost. Cost may also be a factor in your yarn selection. Again, acrylic yarn is a favorite because it is reasonably priced and comes in a wide variety of colors. However, if your project is something extra special, you may want to spend a little more on tapestry yarn or Persian wool yarn to get certain shades of color.

Dye Lot Variations. It is important to buy all of the yarn you need to complete your project from the same dye lot. Although variations in color may be slight when yarns from two different dye lots are held together, the variation is usually apparent on a stitched piece.

Embroidery Floss. Embroidery floss consists of six strands that are twisted together. To ensure smoother stitches, separate the strands of floss and realign them before threading your needle. Unless otherwise noted in the project instructions or color key, use six strands of floss to stitch the projects in this book.

Yarn Colors. Choosing colors can be fun, but sometimes a little difficult. Your project will tell you what yarn colors you will need. When you begin searching for the recommended colors, you may be slightly overwhelmed by the different shades of each color. Here are a few guidelines to consider when choosing your colors.

Consider where you are going to place the finished project. If the project is going in a particular room in your house, match your yarn to the room's colors.

Some projects require several shades of a color, such as shades of red for a Santa. Be sure your shades blend well together.

Sometimes, you may have trouble finding three or four shades of a color. If you think your project warrants the extra expense, you can usually find several shades of a color available in tapestry yarn or Persian wool yarn.

Yarn Yardage Estimator. A handy way of estimating yardage is to make a yarn yardage estimator. Cut a one-yard piece of yarn for each different stitch used in your project. For each stitch, work as many stitches as you can with the one-yard length of yarn.

To use your yarn yardage estimator, count the number of stitches you were able to make, suppose 72 Tent Stitches. Now look at the chart for the project you want to make. Estimate the number of ecru Tent Stitches on the chart, suppose 150. Now divide the estimated number of ecru stitches by the actual number stitched with a yard of yarn. One hundred fifty divided by 72 is approximately two. So you will need about two yards of ecru yarn to make your project. Repeat this for all stitches and yarn colors. To allow for repairs and practice stitches, purchase extra yardage of each color. If you have yarn left over, remember that scraps of yarn are perfect for small projects such as magnets or when you need just a few inches of a particular color for another project.

TYPES OF YARN

Yarn Usage. The first question to ask when choosing yarn is, "How will my project be used?" If your finished project will be handled or used a lot, such as a coaster or magnet, you will want to use a durable, washable yarn. We highly recommend acrylic or nylon yarn for plastic canvas. It can be washed repeatedly and holds up well to frequent usage and handling. If your finished project won't be handled or used frequently, such as a framed picture or a bookend, you are not limited to washable yarns.

The types of yarns available are endless, and each grouping of yarn has its own characteristics and uses. The following is a brief description of some common yarns used for plastic canvas.

Worsted Weight Yarn. This yarn may be found in acrylic, wool, wool blends, and a variety of other fiber contents. Worsted weight yarn is the most popular yarn used for 7 mesh plastic canvas because one strand covers the canvas very well. This yarn is inexpensive and comes in a wide range of colors.

Most brands of worsted weight yarn have four plies that are twisted together to form one strand. When the color key indicates "2-ply," separate the strand of yarn and stitch using only two of the four plies.

Needloft® Yarn will not easily separate. When the instructions call for "2-ply" yarn, we recommend that you substitute with six strands of embroidery floss.

Sport Weight Yarn. This yarn has four thin plies that are twisted together to form one strand. Like worsted weight yarn, sport weight yarn comes in a variety of fiber contents. The color selection in sport weight yarn is more limited than in other types of yarns. You may want to use a double strand of sport weight yarn for better coverage of your 7 mesh canvas. Sport weight yarn works nicely for 10 mesh canvas.

Tapestry Yarn. This is a thin wool yarn. Because tapestry yarn is available in a wider variety of colors than other yarns, it may be used when several shades of the same color are desired. For example, if you need five shades of pink to stitch a flower, you may choose tapestry yarn for a better blending of colors. Tapestry yarn is ideal for

working on 10 mesh canvas. However, it is a more expensive yarn and requires two strands to cover 7 mesh canvas. Projects made with tapestry yarn cannot be washed.

Persian Wool. This is a wool yarn that is made up of three loosely twisted plies. The plies should be separated and realigned before you thread your needle. Like tapestry yarn, Persian yarn has more shades of each color from which to choose. It also has a nap similar to the nap of velvet. To determine the direction of the nap, run the yarn through your fingers. When you rub "with the nap," the yarn feels smooth; but when you rub "against the nap," the yarn feels rough. For smoother and prettier stitches on your project, stitching should be done "with the nap." The yarn fibers will stand out when stitching is done "against the nap." Because of the wool content, you cannot wash projects made with Persian yarn.

Pearl Cotton. Sometimes #3 pearl cotton is used on plastic canvas to give it a dressy, lacy look. It is not meant to cover 7 mesh canvas completely but to enhance it. Pearl cotton works well on 10 mesh canvas when you want your needlework to have a satiny sheen. If you cannot locate #3 pearl cotton in your area, you can substitute with 12 strands of embroidery floss.

SELECTING NEEDLES

Stitching on plastic canvas should be done with a blunt needle called a tapestry needle. Tapestry needles are sized by numbers; the higher the number, the smaller the needle. The correct size needle to use depends on the canvas mesh size and the yarn thickness. The needle should be small enough to allow the threaded needle to pass through the canvas holes easily, without disturbing canvas threads. The eye of the needle should be large enough to allow yarn to be threaded easily. If the eye is too small, the yarn will wear thin and may break. You will find the recommended needle size listed in the supply section of each project. If the supply list for the project you have chosen lists more than one needle size, refer to the chart below to select the correct tapestry needle.

MESH	NEEDLE
7	#16 tapestry
10	#20 tapestry
14	#24 tapestry

WORKING WITH PLASTIC CANVAS

Throughout this book, the lines of the canvas will be referred to as threads. However, they are not actually "threads" since the canvas is nonwoven. To cut plastic canvas pieces accurately, count **threads** (not **holes**) as shown in **Fig. 1**.

Fig. 1

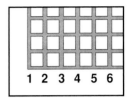

Thread Count. Before cutting your pieces, notice the thread count of each piece on your chart. The thread count is usually located above the piece on the chart. The thread count tells you the number of threads in the width and the height of the canvas piece. Follow the thread count to cut out a rectangle the specified size. Remember to count **threads**, not **holes**. If you accidentally count holes, your piece is going to be the wrong size. Follow the chart to trim the rectangle into the desired shape.

Marking the Canvas. If you find it necessary to mark on the canvas, use an overhead projector pen. Outline shape with pen, cut out shape, and remove markings with a damp paper towel.

Cutting the Canvas. A good pair of household scissors is recommended for cutting plastic canvas. However, a craft knife is helpful when cutting a small area from the center of a larger piece of canvas. For example, a craft knife is recommended for cutting the opening out of a tissue box cover top. When using a craft knife, be sure to protect the table below your canvas. A layer of cardboard or a magazine should provide enough padding to protect your table.

When cutting canvas, be sure to cut as close to the thread as possible without cutting into the thread. If you don't cut close enough, "nubs," or "pickets" will be left on the edge of your canvas. Be sure to cut all nubs from the canvas before you begin to stitch, because nubs will snag the yarn and are difficult to cover.

Continued on page 92

When cutting plastic canvas along a diagonal, cut through the center of each intersection. This will leave enough plastic canvas on both sides of the cut so that both pieces of canvas may be used. Diagonal corners will also snag yarn less and be easier to cover.

If your project has several pieces, you may want to cut them all out before you begin stitching. Keep your cut pieces in a resealable plastic bag to prevent loss.

THREADING YOUR NEEDLE

Many people wonder, "What is the best way to thread my needle?" Here are a couple of methods. Practice each one with a scrap of yarn and see what works best for you. There are also several yarn-size needle threaders available at your local craft store.

Fold Method. First, sharply fold the end of yarn over your needle; then remove needle. Keeping the fold sharp, push the needle onto the yarn (**Fig. 2**).

Fig. 2

Thread Method. Fold a 5" piece of sewing thread in half, forming a loop. Insert loop of thread through the eye of your needle (**Fig. 3**). Insert yarn through the loop and pull the thread back through your needle, pulling yarn through at the same time.

Fig. 3

READING THE COLOR KEY

A color key is included for each project. The key indicates the colors of yarn used and how each color is represented on the chart. For example, when white yarn is represented by a grey line in the color key, all grey stitches on the chart should be stitched using white yarn.

READING THE CHART

Whenever possible, the drawing on the chart looks like the completed stitch. For example, the Tent Stitches on the chart are drawn diagonally across one intersection of threads just like Tent Stitches look on your piece of canvas. Likewise, Gobelin Stitches on the chart look identical to the Gobelin Stitches on your canvas. When a stitch cannot clearly be drawn on the chart, such as a French Knot, a symbol will be used instead. If you have difficulty determining how a particular stitch is worked, refer to Stitch Diagrams, page 93.

STITCHING THE DESIGN

Securing the First Stitch. Don't knot the end of your yarn before you begin stitching. Instead, begin each length of yarn by coming up from the wrong side of the canvas and leaving a 1" - 2" tail on the wrong side. Hold this tail against the canvas and work the first few stitches over the tail. When thread is secure, clip the tail close to your stitched piece. Clipping the tail closely is important because long tails can become tangled in future stitches or show through to the right side of the canvas.

Using Even Tension. Keep your stitching tension consistent, with each stitch lying flat and even on the canvas. Pulling or yanking the yarn causes the tension to be too tight, and you will be able to see through your project. Loose tension is caused by not pulling the yarn firmly enough, and the yarn will not lie flat on the canvas.

Ending Your Stitches. After you've completed all of the stitches of one color in an area, end your stitching by running your needle under several stitches on the back of the stitched piece. To keep the tails of the yarn from showing through or becoming tangled in future stitches, trim the end of the yarn close to the stitched piece.

Stitching Tips

Length of Yarn. It is best to begin stitching with a piece of yarn that is approximately one yard long. However, when working large areas of the same color, you may want to begin with a longer length of yarn to reduce the number of yarn ends and keep the back of your project looking neat.

Keeping Stitches Smooth. Most stitches tend to twist the yarn. Drop your needle and let the yarn untwist every few stitches or whenever needed.

JOINING PIECES

Straight Edges. The most common method of assembling stitched pieces is joining two or more pieces of canvas along a straight edge using Overcast Stitches. Place one piece on top of the other with right or wrong sides together. Make sure the edges being joined are even, then stitch the pieces together through all layers.

Shaded Areas. The shaded area is part of a chart that has colored shading on top of it. Shaded areas usually mean that all the stitches in that area are used to join pieces of canvas. Do not work the stitches in a shaded area until your project instructions say you should.

Stacking. Sometimes pieces need to be thicker than one layer of canvas. You can do this by stacking. Before you begin stitching, follow your project instructions to stack together plastic canvas pieces so that the edges are even.

Tacking. To tack pieces, run your needle under the backs of some stitches on one stitched piece to secure the yarn. Then run your needle through the canvas or under the stitches on the piece to be tacked in place. The idea is to securely attach your pieces without your tacking stitches showing.

Uneven Edges. Sometimes you'll need to join a diagonal edge to a straight edge. The holes of the two pieces will not line up exactly. Just keep the pieces even and stitch through holes as many times as necessary to completely cover the canvas.

Unworked Threads. Sometimes you'll need to join the edge of one piece to an unworked thread in the center of another piece. Simply place one piece on top of the other, matching the indicated threads or symbols. Join by stitching through both layers.

WASHING INSTRUCTIONS

If you used washable yarn for all of your stitches, you may hand-wash plastic canvas projects in warm water with a mild soap. Do not rub or scrub stitches; this will cause the yarn to fuzz. Allow your stitched piece to air dry. Do not put stitched pieces in a clothes dryer. The plastic canvas could melt in the heat of a dryer. Do not dry clean your plastic canvas. The chemicals used in dry cleaning could dissolve the plastic canvas. When piece is dry, you may need to trim the fuzz from your project with a small pair of sharp scissors.

STITCH DIAGRAMS

> Unless otherwise indicated, bring threaded needle up at 1 and all odd numbers and down at 2 and all even numbers.

ALICIA LACE STITCH

This series of stitches is worked in diagonal rows and forms a lacy pattern. Follow **Fig. 4** and work in one direction to cover every other diagonal row of intersections. Then work in the other direction **(Fig. 5)** to cover the remaining intersections.

Fig. 4

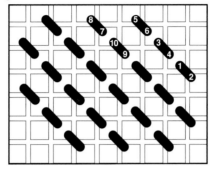

Fig. 5

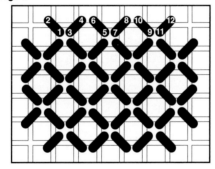

ALTERNATING OVERCAST STITCH

This stitch covers the edge of the canvas and joins pieces of canvas. With first color, work Overcast Stitches in every other hole. Then with second color, work Overcast Stitches in the remaining holes **(Fig. 6)**.

Fig. 6

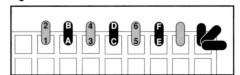

ALTERNATING SCOTCH STITCH

This Scotch Stitch variation is worked over three or more threads, forming alternating blocks **(Fig. 7)**.

Fig. 7

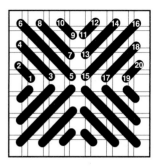

BACKSTITCH

This stitch is worked over completed stitches to outline or define **(Fig. 8)**. It is sometimes worked over more than one thread. Backstitch may also be used to cover canvas as shown in **Fig. 9**.

Fig. 8

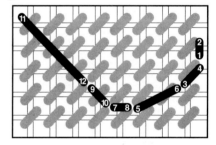

Fig. 9

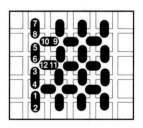

Continued on page 94

CROSS STITCH

This stitch is composed of two stitches **(Fig. 10)**. The top stitch of each cross must always be made in the same direction. The number of intersections may vary according to the chart.

Fig. 10

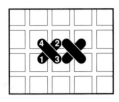

DOUBLE FRENCH KNOT

Bring needle up through hole. Wrap yarn twice around needle and insert needle in same hole or adjacent hole **(Fig. 11)**. Tighten knot; then pull needle through canvas, holding yarn until it must be released.

Fig. 11

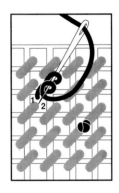

FRENCH KNOT

Bring needle up through hole. Wrap yarn once around needle and insert needle in same hole or adjacent hole, holding end of yarn with non-stitching fingers **(Fig. 12)**. Tighten knot; then pull needle through canvas, holding yarn until it must be released.

Fig. 12

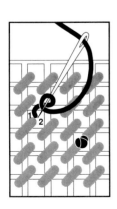

FRINGE STITCH

Go down in hole, leaving a $3/4$" end. Holding end in place with thumb, come up in the same hole, leaving a 1" loop **(Fig. 13)**. Bring loose end and needle through loop **(Fig. 14)** and pull tightly. Trim strands to desired length from knot. A dot of glue on back of Fringe will help keep stitches in place.

Fig. 13

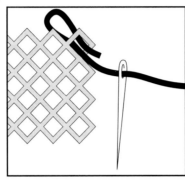

Fig. 14

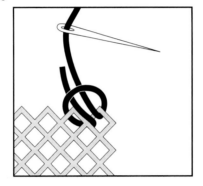

GOBELIN STITCH

This basic straight stitch is worked over two or more threads or intersections. The number of threads or intersections may vary according to the chart **(Fig. 15)**.

Fig. 15

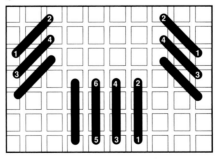

LAZY DAISY STITCH

Bring needle up at 1. Insert needle in same hole, leaving a loop on top of canvas. Bring needle up at 2 and through the loop. To secure loop, insert needle at 2 and gently pull yarn back through canvas until loop lies flat on the canvas **(Fig. 16)**.

Fig. 16

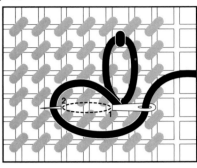

MODIFIED COUCHING STITCH

This stitch is composed of one long stitch held in place by vertical tie-down stitches **(Fig. 17)**.

Fig. 17

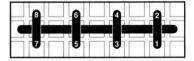

MODIFIED LAZY DAISY STITCH

Bring needle up at 1. Insert needle in same hole, leaving a loop on top of canvas. Bring needle up at 2 and through the loop. To secure loop, insert needle into adjacent hole and gently pull yarn back through canvas until loop lies flat on the canvas **(Fig. 18)**.

Fig. 18

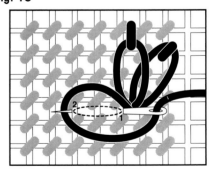

MOSAIC STITCH
This three-stitch pattern forms small squares (**Fig. 19**).

Fig. 19

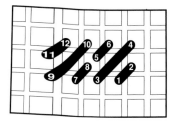

OVERCAST STITCH
This stitch covers the edge of the canvas and joins pieces of canvas (**Fig. 20**). It may be necessary to go through the same hole more than once to get an even coverage on the edge, especially at the corners.

Fig. 20

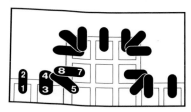

SCOTCH STITCH
This stitch forms a square. It may be worked over three or more horizontal threads by three or more vertical threads. Fig. 21 shows the Scotch Stitch worked over three threads.

Fig. 21

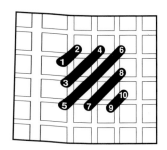

SMYRNA CROSS STITCH
This stitch is worked over two threads as a decorative stitch. Each stitch is worked completely before going on to the next (**Fig. 22**).

Fig. 22

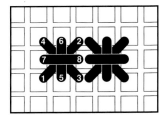

STEM STITCH
This stitch is a series of slanted stitches worked vertically with each row changing direction (**Fig. 23**).

Fig. 23

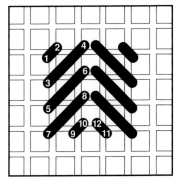

TENT STITCH
This stitch is worked in horizontal or vertical rows over one intersection as shown in **Fig. 24**. Follow **Fig. 25** to work the **Reversed Tent Stitch**. Sometimes when you are working Tent Stitches, the last stitch on the row will look "pulled" on the front of your piece when you are changing directions. To avoid this problem, leave a loop of yarn on the wrong side of the stitched piece after making the last stitch in the row. When making the first stitch in the next row, run your needle through the loop (**Fig. 26**). Gently pull yarn until all stitches are even.

Fig. 24

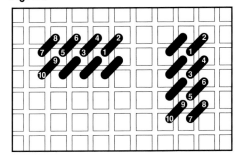

Fig. 25

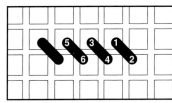

Fig. 26

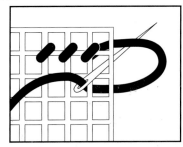

TURKEY LOOP STITCH
This stitch is composed of locked loops. Bring needle up through hole and back down through same hole, forming a loop on top of the canvas. A locking stitch is then made across the thread directly below or to either side of loop as shown in **Fig. 27**.

Fig. 27

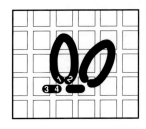

Instructions tested and photography items made by Sharla Dunigan, Michelle E. Goodrich, Carlene Hodge, Lorene K. Polston, Tracy Thomas, and Sadie Wilson.

INDEX